This Journal Belongs to:

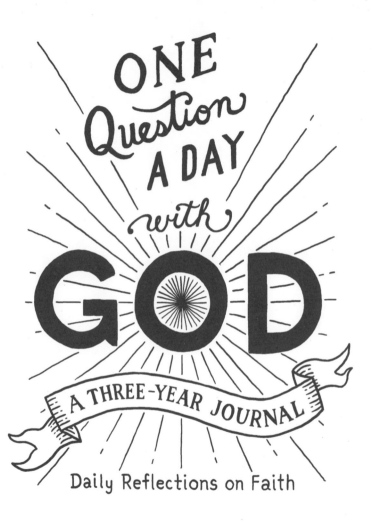

ONE Question A DAY with GOD

A THREE-YEAR JOURNAL

Daily Reflections on Faith

CASTLE POINT BOOKS
NEW YORK

ONE QUESTION A DAY WITH GOD.
Copyright © 2024 by St. Martin's Press.

All rights reserved. Printed in Turkey. For information, address St. Martin's Publishing Group, 120 Broadway, New York, NY 10271.

www.castlepointbooks.com

The Castle Point Books trademark is owned by Castle Point Publishing, LLC.
Castle Point books are published and distributed by St. Martin's Publishing Group.

ISBN 978-1-250-32392-7 (flexibound)

Images used under license from Shutterstock.com

All scripture quotations are taken from the following sources:

Holy Bible, New International Version®, NIV®.
Copyright © 1973, 1978, 1984, 2011 by Biblica, Inc.®
Used by permission. All rights reserved worldwide.

The Holy Bible, English Standard Version. ESV Text Edition: 2016.
Copyright © 2001 by Crossway Bibles, a publishing ministry of Good News Publishers.

New American Standard Bible®,
Copyright © 1960, 1971, 1977, 1995, 2020 by The Lockman Foundation.
All rights reserved.

New Revised Standard Version, Updated Edition.
Copyright © 2021 National Council of Churches of Christ in the United States
of America. Used by permission. All rights reserved worldwide.

Holy Bible, New Living Translation, copyright © 1996, 2004, 2015 by Tyndale House
Foundation. Used by permission of Tyndale House Publishers, Inc., Carol Stream,
Illinois 60188. All rights reserved.

New Century Version®. Copyright © 2005 by Thomas Nelson.
Used by permission. All rights reserved.

New King James Version®. Copyright © 1982 by Thomas Nelson.
Used by permission. All rights reserved.

Our books may be purchased in bulk for promotional, educational, or business use.
Please contact your local bookseller or the Macmillan Corporate and Premium
Sales Department at 1-800-221-7945, extension 5442, or by email at
MacmillanSpecialMarkets@macmillan.com.

First Edition: 2024

10 9 8 7 6 5 4 3 2 1

How to Use This Journal

Journal your way to stronger faith and deeper peace with *One Question a Day with God*. Questions are only natural— part of being human and not always being able to see the greater picture. When you bring your questions to God, you can surrender your anxiety and uncertainty at His feet and grow greater in your trust and closer in your relationship with Him.

No matter how busy you are, using this journal will remind you to look to God for daily inspiration and take time to meditate on the wisdom He provides. It's simple: Open to today's date and add the current year. Read the Scripture selection and the accompanying question, then ask God to guide your answer. Every page of *One Question a Day with God* lets you pause to invite spiritual direction into your life. Notice how your answers evolve year after year and praise the Lord for your faith journey.

God has the answers, so go to Him with the questions! Pair them with prayer, listening, time in Scripture, and discernment, and you will see paths become clearer and you will feel more confident and joyful in your daily faith walk.

January 1

"See, I am doing a new thing!
Now it springs up; do you not perceive it?"
—Isaiah 43:19 (NIV)

Where are You pointing me
toward a fresh start?

Year: _____

_____
_____
_____
_____

Year: _____

_____
_____
_____
_____

Year: _____

_____
_____
_____
_____

January 2

"'Love your neighbor as you love yourself.
I am the LORD.'"
—Leviticus 19:18b (NCV)

Who is the neighbor who most
needs my love today?

Year: _____

_____
_____
_____
_____

Year: _____

_____
_____
_____
_____

Year: _____

_____
_____
_____
_____

January 3

Trust in the LORD with all your heart
and lean not on your own understanding.
—Proverbs 3:5 (NIV)

In what area of my life do I need to stop leaning
on my own understanding?

Year: _____

_____

_____

_____

_____

Year: _____

_____

_____

_____

_____

Year: _____

_____

_____

_____

_____

January 4

Weeping may tarry for the night,
but joy comes with the morning.
—Psalm 30:5b (ESV)

Where will You lead me to joy today?

Year: _____

_____

_____

_____

_____

Year: _____

_____

_____

_____

_____

Year: _____

_____

_____

_____

_____

January 5

Cast all your anxiety on him, because he cares for you.
—1 Peter 5:7 (NRSVUE)

What words of prayer can soothe me
when I need Your calm?

Year: _____

_____
_____
_____
_____

Year: _____

_____
_____
_____
_____

Year: _____

_____
_____
_____
_____

January 6

So now I am glad to boast about my weaknesses, so that
the power of Christ can work through me.
—2 Corinthians 12:9 (NLT)

What weakness or struggle can remind me that
my strength comes from You alone?

Year: _____

_____
_____
_____
_____

Year: _____

_____
_____
_____
_____

Year: _____

_____
_____
_____
_____

January 7

*Therefore, go and make disciples of all the nations, baptizing
them in the name of the Father and the Son and the Holy Spirit.*
—Matthew 28:19 (NLT)

Who is waiting for me to share
the Good News?

Year: _____

_____

_____

_____

_____

Year: _____

_____

_____

_____

_____

Year: _____

_____

_____

_____

_____

January 8

Draw near to God, and he will draw near to you.
—James 4:8a (ESV)

Where I can go today to feel close to You?

Year: _____

_____

_____

_____

_____

Year: _____

_____

_____

_____

_____

Year: _____

_____

_____

_____

_____

January 9

"In the world you have tribulation,
but take courage; I have overcome the world."
—John 16:33b (NASB)

What hard thing can I do because I know
that Jesus has already overcome?

Year: _____

_____

_____

_____

_____

Year: _____

_____

_____

_____

_____

Year: _____

_____

_____

_____

_____

January 10

*Think about things that are excellent
and worthy of praise.*
—Philippians 4:8b (NLT)

Where would You have me direct
my thoughts today?

Year: _____

_____

_____

_____

_____

Year: _____

_____

_____

_____

_____

Year: _____

_____

_____

_____

_____

January 11

For God so loved the world that he gave
his one and only Son, that whoever believes in him
shall not perish but have eternal life.

—John 3:16 (NIV)

Is there anything You see getting in
the way of my belief?

Year: _____

_____

_____

_____

_____

Year: _____

_____

_____

_____

_____

Year: _____

_____

_____

_____

_____

January 12

The LORD is my shepherd;
I have everything I need.
—Psalm 23:1 (NCV)

What am I desiring that will not make my
life any more complete?

Year: _____

_____

_____

_____

_____

Year: _____

_____

_____

_____

_____

Year: _____

_____

_____

_____

_____

January 13

*Let us think of ways to motivate one another
to acts of love and good works.*
—Hebrews 10:24 (NLT)

Who can spur me to produce good fruit
when I need motivation?

Year: _____

_____

_____

_____

_____

Year: _____

_____

_____

_____

_____

Year: _____

_____

_____

_____

_____

January 14

They saw Jesus walking on the sea and coming near the boat, and they were frightened. But he said to them, "It is I; do not be afraid."
—John 6:19–20 (ESV)

In what situation are You walking toward me
and telling me not to be afraid?

Year: _____

_____

_____

_____

_____

Year: _____

_____

_____

_____

_____

Year: _____

_____

_____

_____

_____

January 15

*And we know that for those who love God
all things work together for good, for those who
are called according to his purpose.*

—Romans 8:28 (ESV)

Where have You transformed a mess in my life
into good for Your purpose?

Year: _____

_____

_____

_____

_____

Year: _____

_____

_____

_____

_____

Year: _____

_____

_____

_____

_____

January *16*

"Come to me, all you who are weary and burdened,
and I will give you rest."
—Matthew 11:28 (NIV)

What opportunities to rest have You provided?

Year: _____

_____
_____
_____
_____

Year: _____

_____
_____
_____
_____

Year: _____

_____
_____
_____
_____

January 17

Therefore, my dear brothers and sisters,
stand firm. Let nothing move you.
—1 Corinthians 15:58a (NIV)

Where should I be firmer in my stand?

Year: _____

_____
_____
_____
_____

Year: _____

_____
_____
_____
_____

Year: _____

_____
_____
_____
_____

January 18

*He comforts us in all our troubles so that we
can comfort others. When they are troubled, we will be able
to give them the same comfort God has given us.*
—2 Corinthians 1:4 (NLT)

What experience has given me the gift of relating to and
comforting others facing something similar?

Year: _____

_____
_____
_____
_____

Year: _____

_____
_____
_____
_____

Year: _____

_____
_____
_____
_____

January 19

Do not conform to the pattern of this world, but be
transformed by the renewing of your mind.
—Romans 12:2a (NIV)

What worldly pattern is most difficult
for me to break away from?

Year: _____

_____
_____
_____
_____

Year: _____

_____
_____
_____
_____

Year: _____

_____
_____
_____
_____

January 20

I know what it is to have little, and I know what it is to have plenty.
—Philippians 4:12a (NRSVUE)

What "plenty" in my life am I most thankful for right now?

Year: _____

_____
_____
_____
_____

Year: _____

_____
_____
_____
_____

Year: _____

_____
_____
_____
_____

January 21

Lead me by your truth and teach me,
for you are the God who saves me.
—Psalm 25:5a (NLT)

What are You trying to teach me this week?

Year: _____

_____
_____
_____
_____

Year: _____

_____
_____
_____
_____

Year: _____

_____
_____
_____
_____

January 22

*May the God who gives endurance and encouragement give you the
same attitude of mind toward each other that Christ Jesus had. . .*
—Romans 15:5 (NIV)

Whom do I need to see with a more
Christlike attitude?

Year: _____

_____
_____
_____
_____

Year: _____

_____
_____
_____
_____

Year: _____

_____
_____
_____
_____

January 23

*I long to see you so that I may impart to you
some spiritual gift to make you strong. . .*
—Romans 1:11 (NIV)

What spiritual gift do I have to offer others,
and how can I use it this week?

Year: _____

_____
_____
_____
_____

Year: _____

_____
_____
_____
_____

Year: _____

_____
_____
_____
_____

January 24

And he said: "Truly I tell you, unless you change and become like little children, you will never enter the kingdom of heaven."
—Matthew 18:3 (NIV)

What childlike qualities do I need to work
on to deepen my faith?

Year: _____

_____
_____
_____
_____

Year: _____

_____
_____
_____
_____

Year: _____

_____
_____
_____
_____

January 25

*My dear brothers and sisters, always be
willing to listen and slow to speak.*
—James 1:19a (NCV)

When do I need to be more willing
to listen and slower to speak?

Year: _____

_____
_____
_____
_____

Year: _____

_____
_____
_____
_____

Year: _____

_____
_____
_____
_____

January 26

This is the day the LORD has made.
We will rejoice and be glad in it.
—Psalm 118:24 (NLT)

How can I be more present in the everyday
moments You give me?

Year: _____

_____
_____
_____
_____

Year: _____

_____
_____
_____
_____

Year: _____

_____
_____
_____
_____

January 27

For as we have many members in one body,
but all the members do not have the same function. . .
—Romans 12:4 (NKJV)

In what situation can I make more of an impact
by gathering with other believers?

Year: _____

_____

_____

_____

_____

Year: _____

_____

_____

_____

_____

Year: _____

_____

_____

_____

_____

January 28

I can do all things through him who strengthens me.
—Philippians 4:13 (NRSVUE)

What challenging moment did I face with
confidence this week because of Christ?

Year: _____

_____

_____

_____

_____

Year: _____

_____

_____

_____

_____

Year: _____

_____

_____

_____

_____

January 29

Always be joyful. Pray continually, and give thanks whatever happens. That is what God wants for you in Christ Jesus.
—1 Thessalonians 5:16–18 (NCV)

What can joy look like in my life?

Year: _____
_____
_____
_____
_____

Year: _____
_____
_____
_____
_____

Year: _____
_____
_____
_____
_____

January 30

Do not let the sun go down while you are still angry,
and do not give the devil a foothold.

—Ephesians 4:26b–27 (NIV)

With whom do I need to make amends?

Year: _____

_____

_____

_____

_____

Year: _____

_____

_____

_____

_____

Year: _____

_____

_____

_____

_____

January 31

*Never be lacking in zeal, but keep your spiritual
fervor, serving the Lord.*
—Romans 12:11 (NIV)

How can I be more on fire for You?

Year: _____

_____
_____
_____
_____

Year: _____

_____
_____
_____
_____

Year: _____

_____
_____
_____
_____

February 1

*Seek the Kingdom of God above all else, and live righteously,
and he will give you everything you need.*
—Matthew 6:33 (NLT)

What am I placing above You right now in my life?

Year: _____

_____

_____

_____

_____

Year: _____

_____

_____

_____

_____

Year: _____

_____

_____

_____

_____

February 2

Share with the Lord's people who are in need.
—Romans 12:13a (NIV)

What material possession can I share with
or give to someone in need?

Year: _____

_____
_____
_____
_____

Year: _____

_____
_____
_____
_____

Year: _____

_____
_____
_____
_____

February 3

*Take care that you are not carried away with the error
of lawless people and lose your own stability.*
—2 Peter 3:17b (ESV)

Where am I most at risk of being carried away?

Year: _____

_____

_____

_____

_____

Year: _____

_____

_____

_____

_____

Year: _____

_____

_____

_____

_____

February 4

Love is patient, love is kind. It does not envy,
it does not boast, it is not proud.
—1 Corinthians 13:4 (NIV)

In what relationship do I need to have
more patience and less pride?

Year: _____

_____
_____
_____
_____

Year: _____

_____
_____
_____
_____

Year: _____

_____
_____
_____
_____

February 5

*Every good action and every
perfect gift is from God.*
—James 1:17a (NCV)

What blessing have I overlooked this week?

Year: _____

_____
_____
_____
_____

Year: _____

_____
_____
_____
_____

Year: _____

_____
_____
_____
_____

February 6

You show me the path of life.
—Psalm 16:11a (NRSVUE)

What path are You revealing that will
lead me closer to You?

Year: _____

_____

_____

_____

_____

Year: _____

_____

_____

_____

_____

Year: _____

_____

_____

_____

_____

February 7

For we do not know what to pray for as we ought, but the Spirit himself intercedes for us with groanings too deep for words.
—Romans 8:26 (ESV)

In what situation is the Holy Spirit
covering me through groans?

Year: _____

_____
_____
_____
_____

Year: _____

_____
_____
_____
_____

Year: _____

_____
_____
_____
_____

February 8

*And the peace of God, which surpasses all understanding,
will guard your hearts and your minds in Christ Jesus.*
—Philippians 4:7 (ESV)

What does it feel like for me to
be at peace in You?

Year: _____

_____

_____

_____

_____

Year: _____

_____

_____

_____

_____

Year: _____

_____

_____

_____

_____

February 9

Humble yourselves, therefore, under the mighty hand of God so that at the proper time he may exalt you. . .
—1 Peter 5:6 (ESV)

When have You been pleased with me
for showing humility?

Year: _____

_____
_____
_____
_____

Year: _____

_____
_____
_____
_____

Year: _____

_____
_____
_____
_____

February 10

And let us not grow weary of doing good, for in due season we will reap, if we do not give up.
—Galatians 6:9 (ESV)

How can I renew my energy right now?

Year: _____

_____

_____

_____

_____

Year: _____

_____

_____

_____

_____

Year: _____

_____

_____

_____

_____

February 11

Depend on the LORD in whatever you do,
and your plans will succeed.
—Proverbs 16:3 (NCV)

What plans am I leaving You out of
instead of including You?

Year: _____

_____

_____

_____

_____

Year: _____

_____

_____

_____

_____

Year: _____

_____

_____

_____

_____

February 12

You have not seen Christ, but still you love him. You cannot see him now, but you believe in him.
—1 Peter 1:8a (NCV)

What do I know about Jesus that makes
me see Him and love Him?

Year: _____

_____

_____

_____

_____

Year: _____

_____

_____

_____

_____

Year: _____

_____

_____

_____

_____

February 13

But as for me and my house, we will serve the LORD.
—Joshua 24:15b (ESV)

How can I make a choice to serve
You this week?

Year: _____

_____
_____
_____
_____

Year: _____

_____
_____
_____
_____

Year: _____

_____
_____
_____
_____

February 14

*For God did not send his Son into the world to condemn
the world, but to save the world through him.*
—John 3:17 (NIV)

Who needs my love when I'm
tempted to condemn?

Year: _____

_____
_____
_____
_____

Year: _____

_____
_____
_____
_____

Year: _____

_____
_____
_____

February 15

Always be prepared to give an answer to everyone who asks you to give the reason for the hope that you have.
—1 Peter 3:15b (NIV)

In whom can I plant a seed this week by
sharing my hope in You?

Year: _____

_____

_____

_____

Year: _____

_____

_____

_____

Year: _____

_____

_____

_____

February 16

Keep your lives free from the love of money,
and be satisfied with what you have.
—Hebrews 13:5a (NCV)

How healthy is my relationship with money?

Year: _____

_____
_____
_____
_____

Year: _____

_____
_____
_____
_____

Year: _____

_____
_____
_____
_____

February 17

Be joyful in hope, patient in affliction, faithful in prayer.
—Romans 12:12 (NIV)

How can I be more faithful in prayer?

Year: _____

_____

_____

_____

_____

Year: _____

_____

_____

_____

_____

Year: _____

_____

_____

_____

_____

February 18

Above all, clothe yourselves with love, which binds
us all together in perfect harmony.
—Colossians 3:14 (NLT)

Where do I need Your love to bring everything together
when it feels like it's falling apart?

Year: _____

_____
_____
_____
_____

Year: _____

_____
_____
_____
_____

Year: _____

_____
_____
_____
_____

February 19

*"Be strong and brave. Don't be afraid of them
and don't be frightened, because the Lord your God will
go with you. He will not leave you or forget you."*

—Deuteronomy 31:6 (NCV)

In what battle do I sometimes forget
You are with me?

Year: _____

_____
_____
_____
_____

Year: _____

_____
_____
_____
_____

Year: _____

_____
_____
_____
_____

February 20

Hold on to wisdom, and it will take care of you.
Love it, and it will keep you safe.

—Proverbs 4:6 (NCV)

How can I connect with Your wisdom
on a deeper level?

Year: _____

_____
_____
_____
_____

Year: _____

_____
_____
_____
_____

Year: _____

_____
_____
_____
_____

February 21

Therefore do not worry about tomorrow, for tomorrow will worry about itself. Each day has enough trouble of its own.
—Matthew 6:34 (NIV)

When do I overplan when I
should simply trust?

Year: _____

_____

_____

_____

_____

Year: _____

_____

_____

_____

_____

Year: _____

_____

_____

_____

_____

February 22

Give your burdens to the LORD,
and he will take care of you.
—Psalm 55:22a (NLT)

What pain from my past do I need
to turn over to You?

Year: _____

_____

_____

_____

_____

Year: _____

_____

_____

_____

_____

Year: _____

_____

_____

_____

_____

February 23

*"But blessed is the one who trusts in the Lord,
whose confidence is in him."*
—Jeremiah 17:7 (NIV)

What goals to be the best can I let go of because
the true confidence I need is in You?

Year: _____

_____

_____

_____

_____

Year: _____

_____

_____

_____

_____

Year: _____

_____

_____

_____

_____

February 24

Dear friends, let us love one another,
for love comes from God.
—1 John 4:7a (NIV)

How can I show Your love today?

Year: _____

_____
_____
_____
_____

Year: _____

_____
_____
_____
_____

Year: _____

_____
_____
_____
_____

February 25

We are from God, and whoever knows God listens to us;
but whoever is not from God does not listen to us.

—1 John 4:6a (NIV)

What and whom am I listening to that is
from You? What is not from You?

Year: _____

_____

_____

_____

_____

Year: _____

_____

_____

_____

_____

Year: _____

_____

_____

_____

_____

February 26

The LORD is my light and my salvation—
so why should I be afraid?
—Psalm 27:1a (NLT)

How can I use my questions and doubts
to lead me closer to You?

Year: _____

_____

_____

_____

_____

Year: _____

_____

_____

_____

_____

Year: _____

_____

_____

_____

_____

February 27

For the Spirit God gave us does not make us timid,
but gives us power, love and self-discipline.
—2 Timothy 1:7 (NIV)

Where do I need to show more self-discipline?

Year: _____

_____

_____

_____

_____

Year: _____

_____

_____

_____

_____

Year: _____

_____

_____

_____

_____

February 28

*Do not worry about anything, but pray and ask God
for everything you need, always giving thanks.*
—Philippians 4:6 (NCV)

What part of my life do I tend to hold back
from You in prayer?

Year: _____

_____
_____
_____
_____

Year: _____

_____
_____
_____
_____

Year: _____

_____
_____
_____
_____

March 1

He has made everything beautiful in its time.
—Ecclesiastes 3:11a (NIV)

How can I put greater trust in Your sense of time?

Year: _____

_____
_____
_____
_____

Year: _____

_____
_____
_____
_____

Year: _____

_____
_____
_____
_____

March 2

The heart of man plans his way,
but the Lord establishes his steps.
—Proverbs 16:9 (ESV)

In what situation do I need to stop pretending
that I have it all figured out by myself?

Year: _____

_____

_____

_____

_____

Year: _____

_____

_____

_____

_____

Year: _____

_____

_____

_____

_____

March 3

*But encourage each other every day while
it is "today." Help each other so none of you will become
hardened because sin has tricked you.*

—Hebrew 3:13 (NCV)

Who needs my encouragement today?

Year: _____

_____
_____
_____
_____

Year: _____

_____
_____
_____
_____

Year: _____

_____
_____
_____
_____

March 4

*Even though I walk through the valley of the shadow of death,
I fear no evil, for You are with me. . .*

—Psalm 23:4a (NASB)

What is the darkest valley You have
brought me through?

Year: _____

Year: _____

Year: _____

March 5

You must hold on, so you can do what God wants
and receive what he has promised.
—Hebrews 10:36 (NCV)

Where am I tempted to give up
but need to persevere?

Year: _____

_____

_____

_____

_____

Year: _____

_____

_____

_____

_____

Year: _____

_____

_____

_____

_____

March 6

If the earthly tent we live in is destroyed, we have a building from God, an eternal house in heaven, not built by human hands.

—1 Corinthians 5:1 (NIV)

What will it be like to find
my home in You?

Year: _____

_____

_____

_____

_____

Year: _____

_____

_____

_____

_____

Year: _____

_____

_____

_____

_____

March 7

The heavens declare the glory of God;
the skies proclaim the work of his hands.
—Psalm 19:1 (NIV)

In what natural setting have I felt
Your glory lately?

Year: _____

_____

_____

_____

_____

Year: _____

_____

_____

_____

_____

Year: _____

_____

_____

_____

_____

March 8

*"Whoever does not carry the cross and follow
me cannot be my disciple."*
—Luke 14:27 (NRSVUE)

What has been my biggest step to follow You?

Year: _____

_____
_____
_____
_____

Year: _____

_____
_____
_____
_____

Year: _____

_____
_____
_____
_____

March 9

Make me to know your ways, O Lord;
teach me your paths.
—Psalm 25:4 (ESV)

Where am I facing a decision to follow
Your way or the world's ways?

Year: _____

_____
_____
_____
_____

Year: _____

_____
_____
_____
_____

Year: _____

_____
_____
_____
_____

March 10

Though war break out against me,
even then I will be confident.
—Psalm 27:3b (NIV)

What hurtful words have I been called that
I know are not who You say I am?

Year: _____

_____

_____

_____

_____

Year: _____

_____

_____

_____

_____

Year: _____

_____

_____

_____

_____

March 11

By helping each other with your troubles,
you truly obey the law of Christ.
—Galatians 6:2 (NCV)

Whom can I help through their
troubles right now?

Year: _____

_____
_____
_____
_____

Year: _____

_____
_____
_____
_____

Year: _____

_____
_____
_____
_____

March 12

If I could speak all the languages of earth and of angels, but didn't love others, I would only be a noisy gong or a clanging cymbal.
—1 Corinthians 13:1 (NLT)

When I have fallen into the trap of noise over love?
How can I avoid it next time?

Year: _____

_____

_____

_____

_____

Year: _____

_____

_____

_____

_____

Year: _____

_____

_____

_____

_____

March 13

Trust in the LORD forever,
for the LORD GOD is an everlasting rock.
—Isaiah 26:4 (ESV)

In what area of my life am I not as steady as I could be
because I am not trusting You?

Year: _____

_____
_____
_____
_____

Year: _____

_____
_____
_____
_____

Year: _____

_____
_____
_____
_____

March 14

Let us, then, feel very sure that we can come before
God's throne where there is grace.
—Hebrews 4:16a (NCV)

When am I hesitant to come to You
even though I need You?

Year: _____

_____
_____
_____
_____

Year: _____

_____
_____
_____
_____

Year: _____

_____
_____
_____
_____

March 15

*See to it, brothers and sisters, that none of you has a sinful,
unbelieving heart that turns away from the living God.*
—Hebrews 3:12 (NIV)

Do You see any sin in my heart
that I need to shed?

Year: _____

_____
_____
_____
_____

Year: _____

_____
_____
_____
_____

Year: _____

_____
_____
_____
_____

March 16

The LORD is good to all;
he has compassion on all he has made.
—Psalm 145:9 (NIV)

Whom do I sometimes exclude from Your love
instead of showing compassion and grace?

Year: _____

_____
_____
_____
_____

Year: _____

_____
_____
_____
_____

Year: _____

_____
_____
_____
_____

March 17

*"I am the LORD, the God of all the peoples of the world.
Is anything too hard for me?"*
—Jeremiah 32:27 (NLT)

When did I worry myself sick when
You had me covered all along?

Year: _____

_____

_____

_____

_____

Year: _____

_____

_____

_____

_____

Year: _____

_____

_____

_____

_____

March 18

*Brothers and sisters, all of you should try to follow my example
and to copy those who live the way we showed you.*
—Philippians 3:17 (NCV)

Whose faith journey has something
timely to teach me?

Year: _____

_____

_____

_____

_____

Year: _____

_____

_____

_____

_____

Year: _____

_____

_____

_____

_____

March 19

After He had sent the crowds away, He went up on the mountain by Himself to pray; and when it was evening, He was there alone.
—Matthew 14:23 (NASB)

Whether for an hour or a weekend, where can
I go to retreat with You?

Year: _____

_____

_____

_____

_____

Year: _____

_____

_____

_____

_____

Year: _____

_____

_____

_____

_____

March 20

Whoever gives heed to instruction prospers,
and blessed is the one who trusts in the LORD.
—Proverbs 16:20 (NIV)

What are You telling me to make more
of a priority in my life?

Year: _____

_____
_____
_____
_____

Year: _____

_____
_____
_____
_____

Year: _____

_____
_____
_____
_____

March 21

My heart is steadfast;
I will sing and make music.
—Psalm 57:7b (NIV)

How can I make music for You,
literally or figuratively?

Year: _____

_____

_____

_____

_____

Year: _____

_____

_____

_____

_____

Year: _____

_____

_____

_____

_____

March 22

Remember the miracles he has done,
his wonders, and his decisions.
—1 Chronicles 16:12 (NCV)

What can I carry with me as a reminder of
Your goodness and my faith in You?

Year: _____

_____

_____

_____

_____

Year: _____

_____

_____

_____

_____

Year: _____

_____

_____

_____

_____

March 23

Let all that you do be done in love.
—1 Corinthians 16:14 (ESV)

In what simple ways can I add
more love to my day?

Year: _____

_____

_____

_____

_____

Year: _____

_____

_____

_____

_____

Year: _____

_____

_____

_____

_____

March 24

*For I am the LORD your God
who takes hold of your right hand...*
—Isaiah 41:13a (NIV)

When do I often lament that I feel alone
although You're right there?

Year: _____

_____
_____
_____
_____

Year: _____

_____
_____
_____
_____

Year: _____

_____
_____
_____

March 25

Our help is in the name of the LORD,
who made heaven and earth.

—Psalm 124:8 (ESV)

Where have You allowed me to see glimpses
of heaven on earth?

Year: _____

_____
_____
_____
_____

Year: _____

_____
_____
_____
_____

Year: _____

_____
_____
_____
_____

March 26

Therefore, if anyone is in Christ, he is a new creation.
The old has passed away; behold, the new has come.
—2 Corinthians 5:17 (ESV)

What is a good title for the story of how You
have changed my life in the past year?

Year: _____

_____

_____

_____

_____

Year: _____

_____

_____

_____

_____

Year: _____

_____

_____

_____

_____

March 27

Don't you realize that your body is the temple of the Holy Spirit, who lives in you and was given to you by God?
—1 Corinthians 6:19a (NLT)

How can I treat my body more like Your temple?

Year: _____

_____

_____

_____

_____

Year: _____

_____

_____

_____

_____

Year: _____

_____

_____

_____

_____

March 28

"But the Helper, the Holy Spirit . . . will teach you all things and bring to your remembrance all that I have said to you."
—John 14:26 (ESV)

When did I miss a nudge from the Holy Spirit?

Year: _____

_____

_____

_____

_____

Year: _____

_____

_____

_____

_____

Year: _____

_____

_____

_____

_____

March 29

He heals the brokenhearted
and binds up their wounds.
—Psalm 147:3 (ESV)

Whose broken heart can I guide to You?

Year: _____

_____
_____
_____
_____

Year: _____

_____
_____
_____
_____

Year: _____

_____
_____
_____
_____

March 30

*Honor the LORD with your wealth
and with the best part of everything you produce.*
—Proverbs 3:9 (NLT)

How am I honoring You with my best?

Year: _____

_____
_____
_____
_____

Year: _____

_____
_____
_____
_____

Year: _____

_____
_____
_____
_____

March 31

I go to bed and sleep in peace,
because, LORD, only you keep me safe.
—Psalm 4:8 (NCV)

How I can be sure to end the day
in Your peace?

Year: _____

_____
_____
_____
_____

Year: _____

_____
_____
_____
_____

Year: _____

_____
_____
_____
_____

April 1

The wise will inherit honor,
but fools get disgrace.
—Proverbs 3:35 (ESV)

When has Your wisdom come to my rescue?

Year: _____

_____

_____

_____

_____

Year: _____

_____

_____

_____

_____

Year: _____

_____

_____

_____

_____

April 2

Therefore, as you received Christ Jesus the Lord, so walk in him, rooted and built up in him and established in the faith. . .
—Colossians 2:6–7a (ESV)

Who helps me stay rooted in Christ?

Year: _____

_____

_____

_____

_____

Year: _____

_____

_____

_____

_____

Year: _____

_____

_____

_____

_____

April 3

*Do not neglect to show hospitality to strangers, for thereby
some have entertained angels unawares.*
—Hebrews 13:2 (ESV)

How can I show hospitality to everyday angels?

Year: _____

_____

_____

_____

_____

Year: _____

_____

_____

_____

_____

Year: _____

_____

_____

_____

_____

April 4

You will seek me and find me when you
seek me with all your heart.
—Jeremiah 29:13 (NIV)

What holds me back from seeking You?

Year: _____

_____

_____

_____

_____

Year: _____

_____

_____

_____

_____

Year: _____

_____

_____

_____

_____

April 5

In all your ways acknowledge him,
and he will make straight your paths.
—Proverbs 3:6 (NRSVUE)

What decision do I need to accept?

Year: _____

_____

_____

_____

_____

Year: _____

_____

_____

_____

_____

Year: _____

_____

_____

_____

_____

April 6

Therefore, since we have such a hope,
we are very bold.
—2 Corinthians 3:12 (NIV)

Where do You need me to be bolder for You?

Year: _____

_____
_____
_____
_____

Year: _____

_____
_____
_____
_____

Year: _____

_____
_____
_____
_____

April 7

*Jesus Christ is the same yesterday
and today and forever.*
—Hebrews 13:8 (NIV)

Through what stressful changes in my life
can I turn to this truth?

Year: _____

_____
_____
_____
_____

Year: _____

_____
_____
_____
_____

Year: _____

_____
_____
_____
_____

April 8

Then our mouth was filled with laughter,
and our tongue with shouts of joy. . .
—Psalm 126:2a (ESV)

How can I invite more laughter into my life?

Year: _____

_____
_____
_____
_____

Year: _____

_____
_____
_____
_____

Year: _____

_____
_____
_____
_____

April 9

Oh give thanks to the LORD; call upon his name;
make known his deeds among the peoples!
—Psalm 105:1 (ESV)

What names do I call You that make
me feel closest to You?

Year: _____

_____
_____
_____
_____

Year: _____

_____
_____
_____
_____

Year: _____

_____
_____
_____
_____

April 10

Forgetting what lies behind . . . I press on toward the goal for the prize of the upward call of God in Christ Jesus.
—Philippians 3:13b–14 (ESV)

What mistake did You help me make
right and move beyond?

Year: _____

_____

_____

_____

_____

Year: _____

_____

_____

_____

_____

Year: _____

_____

_____

_____

_____

April 11

Keep using the gift God gave you when I laid my hands on you.
Now let it grow, as a small flame grows into a fire.
—2 Timothy 1:6 (NCV)

∾⌇∾

When do I feel on fire with purpose for You?

Year: _____

_____
_____
_____
_____

Year: _____

_____
_____
_____
_____

Year: _____

_____
_____
_____
_____

April 12

Set your mind on things above,
not on things on the earth.
—Colossians 3:2 (NKJV)

When am I tempted to measure my efforts by the
world's standards instead of Yours?

Year: _____

_____
_____
_____
_____

Year: _____

_____
_____
_____
_____

Year: _____

_____
_____
_____
_____

April 13

As iron sharpens iron,
so a friend sharpens a friend.
—Proverbs 27:17 (NLT)

Who have You clearly placed in my life?

Year: _____

_____

_____

_____

_____

Year: _____

_____

_____

_____

_____

Year: _____

_____

_____

_____

_____

April 14

The LORD is good to those who wait for him,
to the soul that seeks him.
—Lamentations 3:25 (NRSVUE)

How can I get better at waiting?

Year: _____

_____

_____

_____

_____

Year: _____

_____

_____

_____

_____

Year: _____

_____

_____

_____

_____

April 15

"Let your word be 'Yes, Yes' or 'No, No'; anything more than this comes from the evil one."
—Matthew 5:37 (NRSVUE)

What should I simply say *no* to today?

Year: _____

_____

_____

_____

_____

Year: _____

_____

_____

_____

_____

Year: _____

_____

_____

_____

_____

April 16

May those who love your salvation
say continually, "Great is the LORD!"
—Psalm 40:16b (ESV)

What praise do I feel for You
in my heart right now?

Year: _____

_____
_____
_____
_____

Year: _____

_____
_____
_____
_____

Year: _____

_____
_____
_____
_____

April 17

"Be strong and courageous. Do not be afraid; do not be discouraged, for the LORD your God will be with you wherever you go."
—Joshua 1:9b (NIV)

When have I accomplished something that could only happen through Your strength?

Year: _____

_____
_____
_____
_____

Year: _____

_____
_____
_____
_____

Year: _____

_____
_____
_____
_____

April 18

"'Do not seek revenge or bear a grudge against anyone among your people, but love your neighbor as yourself.'"
—Leviticus 19:18a (NIV)

What grudge or desire for revenge
do I need to let go?

Year: _____

_____

_____

_____

_____

Year: _____

_____

_____

_____

_____

Year: _____

_____

_____

_____

_____

April 19

When you talk, do not say harmful things, but say what people need—words that will help others become stronger.
—Ephesians 4:29a (NCV)

What good words do You want me to speak
to someone in my life?

Year: _____

_____

_____

_____

_____

Year: _____

_____

_____

_____

_____

Year: _____

_____

_____

_____

_____

April 20

But grow in the grace and knowledge of our Lord and Savior Jesus Christ. Glory be to him now and forever! Amen.

—2 Peter 3:18 (NCV)

How do You see me growing in my faith?

Year: _____

_____

_____

_____

_____

Year: _____

_____

_____

_____

_____

Year: _____

_____

_____

_____

_____

April 21

Live the kind of life that honors and pleases the Lord in every way.
—Colossians 1:10a (NCV)

What is missing from my life that You are longing for me to add?

Year: _____

_____
_____
_____
_____

Year: _____

_____
_____
_____
_____

Year: _____

_____
_____
_____
_____

April 22

But if you bite and devour one another,
beware lest you be consumed by one another!
—Galatians 5:15 (NKJV)

From what drama do I need to
simply walk away?

Year: _____

_____

_____

_____

_____

Year: _____

_____

_____

_____

_____

Year: _____

_____

_____

_____

_____

April 23

*After the earthquake came a fire, but the LORD was not
in the fire. And after the fire came a gentle whisper.*
—1 Kings 19:12 (NIV)

In what (sometimes surprising) everyday
sensations can I feel You?

Year: _____

_____

_____

_____

_____

Year: _____

_____

_____

_____

_____

Year: _____

_____

_____

_____

_____

April 24

I asked the angel who was talking with me, "My lord, what do these horses mean?" "I will show you," the angel replied.
—Zechariah 1:9 (NLT)

When do I need to simply ask You to
show me Your meaning?

Year: _____

_____

_____

_____

_____

Year: _____

_____

_____

_____

_____

Year: _____

_____

_____

_____

_____

April 25

For we are God's handiwork, created in Christ Jesus to do good works, which God prepared in advance for us to do.
—Ephesians 2:10 (NIV)

Where have I seen faith-inspired action
in the news recently?

Year: _____

_____
_____
_____
_____

Year: _____

_____
_____
_____
_____

Year: _____

_____
_____
_____
_____

April 26

But the Spirit produces the fruit of love, joy, peace, patience, kindness, goodness, faithfulness, gentleness, self-control.
—Galatians 5:22–23a (NCV)

What fruit do I need more of in my life?
How would it help me?

Year: _____

_____
_____
_____
_____

Year: _____

_____
_____
_____
_____

Year: _____

_____
_____
_____
_____

April 27

God is our refuge and strength,
an ever-present help in trouble.
—Psalm 46:1 (NIV)

How can I remind myself throughout
the day that I am safe in You?

Year: _____

_____
_____
_____
_____

Year: _____

_____
_____
_____
_____

Year: _____

_____
_____
_____
_____

April 28

Give me an undivided heart,
that I may fear your name.
—Psalm 86:11b (NIV)

What is tugging my time and
attention away from You?

Year: _____

_____
_____
_____
_____

Year: _____

_____
_____
_____
_____

Year: _____

_____
_____
_____
_____

April 29

God called you to be free, but do not use your freedom as an excuse
to do what pleases your sinful self. Serve each other with love.
—Galatians 5:13 (NCV)

Where am I crossing the line in my freedom,
and where am I serving?

Year: _____

_____
_____
_____
_____

Year: _____

_____
_____
_____
_____

Year: _____

_____
_____
_____
_____

April 30

The LORD is my strength and my song;
he has become my salvation.
—Psalm 118:14 (ESV)

What song can I use to center me in
Your goodness and grace?

Year: _____

_____

_____

_____

_____

Year: _____

_____

_____

_____

_____

Year: _____

_____

_____

_____

_____

May 1

"You are the salt of the earth, but if salt has lost its taste, how can its saltiness be restored?"
—Matthew 5:13 (NRSVUE)

How can I be sure to keep my saltiness?

Year: _____

_____
_____
_____
_____

Year: _____

_____
_____
_____
_____

Year: _____

_____
_____
_____
_____

May 2

The LORD says, "My thoughts are not like your thoughts.
Your ways are not like my ways."
—Isaiah 55:8 (NCV)

In what situation would it be a relief to
admit I'm not in control?

Year: _____

_____

_____

_____

_____

Year: _____

_____

_____

_____

_____

Year: _____

_____

_____

_____

_____

May 3

Without wood, a fire will go out,
and without gossip, quarreling will stop.
—Proverbs 26:20 (NCV)

How can I avoid the temptation to gossip
and call it out when I hear it?

Year: _____

_____

_____

_____

_____

Year: _____

_____

_____

_____

_____

Year: _____

_____

_____

_____

_____

May 4

For since the creation of the world God's invisible qualities . . . have been clearly seen, being understood from what has been made. . .
—Romans 1:20a (NIV)

How has my understanding of You
changed in the past year?

Year: _____

_____
_____
_____
_____

Year: _____

_____
_____
_____
_____

Year: _____

_____
_____
_____
_____

May 5

"Blessed are the peacemakers, for they will be called children of God."
—Matthew 5:9 (NRSVUE)

In what situation can I be a peacemaker?

Year: _____

_____

_____

_____

_____

Year: _____

_____

_____

_____

_____

Year: _____

_____

_____

_____

_____

May 6

"If you had faith even as small as a mustard seed, you could say to this mountain, 'Move from here to there,' and it would move..."
—Matthew 17:20b (NLT)

What is simple that I tend to overcomplicate?

Year: _____

Year: _____

Year: _____

May 7

*He holds in his hands the depths of the earth
and the mightiest mountains.*
—Psalm 95:4 (NLT)

What remarkable sight made me recently
pause in awe of Your glory?

Year: _____

_____

_____

_____

_____

Year: _____

_____

_____

_____

_____

Year: _____

_____

_____

_____

_____

May 8

Put your hope in God,
for I will yet praise him. . .
—Psalm 42:5b (NIV)

In what situation do I need renewed hope?

Year: _____

_____
_____
_____
_____

Year: _____

_____
_____
_____
_____

Year: _____

_____
_____
_____
_____

May 9

*The LORD has given them special skills as engravers,
designers, embroiderers in blue, purple, and scarlet
thread on fine linen cloth, and weavers.*
—Exodus 35:35a (NLT)

How can I use my creative talents
to bring You glory?

Year: _____

_____

_____

_____

_____

Year: _____

_____

_____

_____

_____

Year: _____

_____

_____

_____

_____

May 10

O LORD, what a variety of things you have made!
In wisdom you have made them all.

—Psalm 104:24a (NLT)

What creatures make me smile
and give You praise?

Year: _____

_____

_____

_____

_____

Year: _____

_____

_____

_____

_____

Year: _____

_____

_____

_____

_____

May 11

*And He said to them, "Go into all the world
and preach the gospel to all creation."*
—Mark 16:15 (NASB)

What one step can I take today to
share Your Good News?

Year: _____

_____

_____

_____

_____

Year: _____

_____

_____

_____

_____

Year: _____

_____

_____

_____

_____

May 12

Fools quickly show that they are upset,
but the wise ignore insults.
—Proverbs 12:16 (NCV)

❧✦❧

How can I become less reactive and take
things less personally?

Year: _____

_____
_____
_____
_____

Year: _____

_____
_____
_____
_____

Year: _____

_____
_____
_____
_____

May 13

I will be your God throughout your lifetime—
until your hair is white with age.
—Isaiah 46:4a (NLT)

How did I see You when I was younger versus now?

Year: _____

_____
_____
_____
_____

Year: _____

_____
_____
_____
_____

Year: _____

_____
_____
_____
_____

May 14

*I praise you, for I am fearfully
and wonderfully made.*
—Psalm 139:14a (ESV)

What physical activity makes me grateful
for my earthly body?

Year: _____

_____

_____

_____

_____

Year: _____

_____

_____

_____

_____

Year: _____

_____

_____

_____

_____

May 15

Say not, "Why were the former days better than these?"
For it is not from wisdom that you ask this.
—Ecclesiastes 7:10 (ESV)

What past dream or idea do I need to release
to make space for a new vision from You?

Year: _____

_____
_____
_____
_____

Year: _____

_____
_____
_____
_____

Year: _____

_____
_____
_____
_____

May 16

Do everything without complaining and arguing,
so that no one can criticize you.
—Philippians 2:14–15a (NLT)

What chore or work can I do without grumbling
and with energy for You?

Year: _____

_____

_____

_____

_____

Year: _____

_____

_____

_____

_____

Year: _____

_____

_____

_____

_____

May 17

"People judge by outward appearance,
but the LORD looks at the heart."

—1 Samuel 16:7b (NLT)

What do You see in my heart?

Year: _____

_____
_____
_____
_____

Year: _____

_____
_____
_____
_____

Year: _____

_____
_____
_____
_____

May 18

Do nothing from selfish ambition or empty conceit, but in humility regard others as better than yourselves.
—Philippians 2:3 (NRSVUE)

How can I show humility today?

Year: _____

_____

_____

_____

_____

Year: _____

_____

_____

_____

_____

Year: _____

_____

_____

_____

_____

May 19

*The night is almost gone, and the day is near. Therefore let's rid
ourselves of the deeds of darkness and put on the armor of light.*
—Romans 13:12 (NASB)

What do I need to consider with more Kingdom
(and less earthly) perspective?

Year: _____

_____

_____

_____

_____

Year: _____

_____

_____

_____

_____

Year: _____

_____

_____

_____

_____

May 20

Heal me, O Lord, and I shall be healed;
save me, and I shall be saved. . .
—Jeremiah 17:14a (ESV)

When have I felt Your healing power?

Year: _____

_____

_____

_____

_____

Year: _____

_____

_____

_____

_____

Year: _____

_____

_____

_____

_____

May 21

But they delight in the law of the LORD,
meditating on it day and night.
—Psalm 1:2 (NLT)

In what area of my home do I find
the most quiet for You?

Year: _____

_____

_____

_____

_____

Year: _____

_____

_____

_____

_____

Year: _____

_____

_____

_____

_____

May 22

*Restore to me the joy of your salvation,
and make me willing to obey you.*
—Psalm 51:12 (NLT)

How can I feel re-energized in You
when I'm struggling?

Year: _____

_____

_____

_____

_____

Year: _____

_____

_____

_____

_____

Year: _____

_____

_____

_____

_____

May 23

*Be kind to one another, compassionate, forgiving each other,
just as God in Christ also has forgiven you.*
—Ephesians 4:32 (NASB)

Who needs a more Christlike approach from me?

Year: _____

_____

_____

_____

_____

Year: _____

_____

_____

_____

_____

Year: _____

_____

_____

_____

_____

May 24

*Examine yourselves to see if your faith
is genuine. Test yourselves.*

—2 Corinthians 13:5a (NLT)

How do I test my faith?

Year: _____

_____

_____

_____

_____

Year: _____

_____

_____

_____

_____

Year: _____

_____

_____

_____

_____

May 25

Teach and counsel each other with all the wisdom he gives. Sing psalms and hymns and spiritual songs to God with thankful hearts.
—Colossians 3:16b (NLT)

Where do I find an encouraging Christian community?

Year: _____

_____

_____

_____

_____

Year: _____

_____

_____

_____

_____

Year: _____

_____

_____

_____

_____

May 26

*Having then gifts differing according to the grace
that is given to us, let us use them. . .*
—Romans 12:6a (NKJV)

What gift could I use more fully for Your glory?

Year: _____

_____
_____
_____
_____

Year: _____

_____
_____
_____
_____

Year: _____

_____
_____
_____
_____

May 27

Taste and see that the LORD is good.
Oh, the joys of those who take refuge in him!
—Psalm 34:8 (NLT)

When have I tasted Your goodness lately?

Year: _____

_____
_____
_____
_____

Year: _____

_____
_____
_____
_____

Year: _____

_____
_____
_____
_____

May 28

*I will meditate on your precepts
and fix my eyes on your ways.*
—Psalm 119:15 (ESV)

How can I better deal with
worldly distractions?

Year: _____

_____
_____
_____
_____

Year: _____

_____
_____
_____
_____

Year: _____

_____
_____
_____
_____

May 29

Don't let anyone think less of you because you are young.
—1 Timothy 4:12a (NLT)

What younger person can
I encourage today?

Year: _____

_____
_____
_____
_____

Year: _____

_____
_____
_____
_____

Year: _____

_____
_____
_____
_____

May 30

*Pray in the Spirit at all times and
on every occasion.*
—Ephesians 6:18a (NLT)

What is an unusual (to the outside world)
prayer I have lifted up recently?

Year: _____

_____
_____
_____
_____

Year: _____

_____
_____
_____
_____

Year: _____

_____
_____
_____
_____

May 31

Then I heard the Lord's voice, saying,
"Whom can I send? Who will go for us?"
So I said, "Here I am. Send me!"

—Isaiah 6:8 (NCV)

What call from You can I answer with a *yes*?

Year: _____

_____

_____

_____

_____

Year: _____

_____

_____

_____

_____

Year: _____

_____

_____

_____

_____

June 1

If he has done anything wrong to you or if he owes you anything, charge that to me.
—Philemon 1:18 (NCV)

Who needs a second chance?

Year: _____

_____

_____

_____

_____

Year: _____

_____

_____

_____

_____

Year: _____

_____

_____

_____

_____

June 2

All Scripture is God-breathed and is useful for teaching, rebuking, correcting and training in righteousness. . .
—2 Timothy 3:16 (NIV)

What are some powerful ways I can interact with Your word?

Year: _____

_____

_____

_____

_____

Year: _____

_____

_____

_____

_____

Year: _____

_____

_____

_____

_____

June 3

*Jesus answered, "I am the way, and the truth, and the life.
The only way to the Father is through me."*
—John 14:6 (NCV)

When do I sometimes try ways other
than through Jesus?

Year: _____

_____
_____
_____
_____

Year: _____

_____
_____
_____
_____

Year: _____

_____
_____
_____
_____

June 4

*Now faith is the assurance of things hoped for,
the conviction of things not seen.*
—Hebrews 11:1 (NRSVUE)

What do I need to give up on trying to
see and just believe?

Year: _____

_____

_____

_____

_____

Year: _____

_____

_____

_____

_____

Year: _____

_____

_____

_____

_____

June 5

Therefore be imitators of God, as beloved children. And walk in love, as Christ loved us and gave himself up for us. . .
—Ephesians 5:1–2 (ESV)

How can I walk in love today?

Year: _____

_____

_____

_____

_____

Year: _____

_____

_____

_____

_____

Year: _____

_____

_____

_____

_____

June 6

*"These things I have spoken to you, that my joy may
be in you, and that your joy may be full."*
—John 15:11 (ESV)

What everyday blessings bring me joy?

Year: _____

_____
_____
_____
_____

Year: _____

_____
_____
_____
_____

Year: _____

_____
_____
_____
_____

June 7

*He has filled the hungry with good things
but has sent the rich away empty.*
—Luke 1:53 (NIV)

Who is physically or emotionally
hungry that I can feed?

Year: _____

_____

_____

_____

_____

Year: _____

_____

_____

_____

_____

Year: _____

_____

_____

_____

_____

June 8

O LORD, you have searched me and known me!
—Psalm 139:1 (ESV)

What surprising things have You revealed
to me about myself?

Year: _____

_____

_____

_____

_____

Year: _____

_____

_____

_____

_____

Year: _____

_____

_____

_____

_____

June 9

God is faithful, and he will not let you be tested beyond your strength, but with the testing he will also provide the way out. . .
—1 Corinthians 10:13b (NRSVUE)

What is Your way out of my most trying situation right now?

Year: _____

_____

_____

_____

_____

Year: _____

_____

_____

_____

_____

Year: _____

_____

_____

_____

_____

June 10

Whatever you ask in my name, this I will do,
that the Father may be glorified in the Son. If you ask
me anything in my name, I will do it.
—John 14:13–14 (ESV)

What big dream have I been hesitant
to bring to You?

Year: _____

_____

_____

_____

_____

Year: _____

_____

_____

_____

_____

Year: _____

_____

_____

_____

_____

June 11

Whoever isolates himself seeks his own desire;
he breaks out against all sound judgment.
—Proverbs 18:1 (ESV)

When do I tend to isolate myself, and how
can I guard against it?

Year: _____

_____
_____
_____
_____

Year: _____

_____
_____
_____
_____

Year: _____

_____
_____
_____
_____

June 12

*Aim for restoration, comfort one another, agree with one another,
live in peace; and the God of love and peace will be with you.*
—2 Corinthians 13:11b (ESV)

When did I feel Your peace today?

Year: _____

_____

_____

_____

_____

Year: _____

_____

_____

_____

_____

Year: _____

_____

_____

_____

_____

June 13

And when you turn to the right or when you turn to the left, your ears shall hear a word behind you, saying, "This is the way; walk in it."
—Isaiah 30:21 (NRSVUE)

In what recent decision did I feel You with me?

Year: _____

_____
_____
_____
_____

Year: _____

_____
_____
_____
_____

Year: _____

_____
_____
_____
_____

June 14

And my God will supply every need of yours according to his riches in glory in Christ Jesus.
—Philippians 4:19 (ESV)

When am I tempted to rely on my own ways
to secure what I think I need?

Year: _____

_____
_____
_____
_____

Year: _____

_____
_____
_____
_____

Year: _____

_____
_____
_____
_____

June 15

A wise person will hear and increase in learning,
And a person of understanding will acquire wise counsel. . .
—Proverbs 1:5 (NASB)

How can I increase my learning and
understanding of You?

Year: _____

_____
_____
_____
_____

Year: _____

_____
_____
_____
_____

Year: _____

_____
_____
_____
_____

June *16*

*And if one member suffers, all the members suffer with it;
or if one member is honored, all the members rejoice with it.*
—1 Corinthians 12:26 (NKJV)

Who can I celebrate and rejoice with today?

Year: _____

_____
_____
_____
_____

Year: _____

_____
_____
_____
_____

Year: _____

_____
_____
_____
_____

June 17

*"Just as you sent me into the world, I am
sending them into the world."*
—John 17:18 (NLT)

Where are You sending me on a mission?

Year: _____

_____
_____
_____
_____

Year: _____

_____
_____
_____
_____

Year: _____

_____
_____
_____
_____

June 18

Do not stifle the Holy Spirit.
—1 Thessalonians 5:19 (NLT)

⌒⌣⌒

In what area of my life am I still
trying to hold back?

Year: _____

_____

_____

_____

_____

Year: _____

_____

_____

_____

_____

Year: _____

_____

_____

_____

_____

June 19

"The Spirit of God created me,
and the breath of the Almighty gave me life."
—Job 33:4 (NCV)

When have You reminded me
to just breathe?

Year: _____

_____

_____

_____

_____

Year: _____

_____

_____

_____

_____

Year: _____

_____

_____

_____

_____

June 20

Let your steadfast love become my comfort
according to your promise to your servant.
—Psalm 119:76 (NRSVUE)

❧❧

What comfort (big or little) do I need right now?

Year: _____

_____
_____
_____
_____

Year: _____

_____
_____
_____
_____

Year: _____

_____
_____
_____
_____

June 21

Whoever is of God hears the words of God.
—John 8:47a (ESV)

When have I heard Your voice
clearly in the past year?

Year: _____

_____
_____
_____
_____

Year: _____

_____
_____
_____
_____

Year: _____

_____
_____
_____
_____

June 22

A cheerful heart is a good medicine,
but a downcast spirit dries up the bones.
—Proverbs 17:22 (NRSVUE)

In what situation could I have a more cheerful heart?

Year: _____

_____

_____

_____

_____

Year: _____

_____

_____

_____

_____

Year: _____

_____

_____

_____

_____

June 23

For I am not ashamed of the gospel; it is God's saving power for everyone who believes. . .
—Romans 1:16a (NRSVUE)

How comfortable am I telling others about
Your power in my life?

Year: _____

_____
_____
_____
_____

Year: _____

_____
_____
_____
_____

Year: _____

_____
_____
_____
_____

June 24

Do not withhold good from those to whom it is due,
when it is in your power to do it.
—Proverbs 3:27 (ESV)

Whom can I bless with my abundance?

Year: _____

_____

_____

_____

_____

Year: _____

_____

_____

_____

_____

Year: _____

_____

_____

_____

_____

June 25

*Speaking the truth with love, we will grow up in every
way into Christ, who is the head.*
—Ephesians 4:15b (NCV)

What changes do I need to make to grow
into a better witness for You?

Year: _____

_____
_____
_____
_____

Year: _____

_____
_____
_____
_____

Year: _____

_____
_____
_____
_____

June 26

"'Now, why wait any longer? Get up, be baptized, and wash your sins away, trusting in him to save you.'"
—Acts 22:16 (NCV)

How can I stop waiting and instead take action?

Year: _____

_____

_____

_____

_____

Year: _____

_____

_____

_____

_____

Year: _____

_____

_____

_____

_____

June 27

Now may the God of peace . . . equip you with
everything good for doing his will. . .
—Hebrews 13:20–21a (NIV)

Are there times that I feel too inexperienced to
do what You need me to do?

Year: _____

_____
_____
_____
_____

Year: _____

_____
_____
_____
_____

Year: _____

_____
_____
_____
_____

June 28

The LORD is near to all who call on him,
to all who call on him in truth.
—Psalm 145:18 (NRSVUE)

When do I struggle with feeling distant from You?

Year: _____

_____
_____
_____
_____

Year: _____

_____
_____
_____
_____

Year: _____

_____
_____
_____
_____

June 29

"Even though you intended to do harm to me, God intended it for good, in order to preserve a numerous people, as he is doing today."
—Genesis 50:20 (NRSVUE)

When have You surprised me with the good
You brought out of a bad situation?

Year: _____

_____
_____
_____
_____

Year: _____

_____
_____
_____
_____

Year: _____

_____
_____
_____
_____

June 30

*See what love the Father has given us, that we should be
called children of God, and that is what we are.*
—1 John 3:1a (NRSVUE)

❧

Who do You say I am despite how
I may feel sometimes?

Year: _____

_____

_____

_____

_____

Year: _____

_____

_____

_____

_____

Year: _____

_____

_____

_____

_____

July 1

"For the Lamb in the midst of the throne will be their shepherd, and he will guide them to springs of living water. . ."
—Revelation 7:17a (ESV)

What have You made known about
our hope in heaven?

Year: _____

_____

_____

_____

_____

Year: _____

_____

_____

_____

_____

Year: _____

_____

_____

_____

_____

July 2

There is a time for everything,
and everything on earth has its special season.
—Ecclesiastes 3:1 (NCV)

What season of my faith am I in right now?

Year: _____

_____
_____
_____
_____

Year: _____

_____
_____
_____
_____

Year: _____

_____
_____
_____
_____

July 3

Humble yourselves in the presence of the Lord,
and He will exalt you.
—James 4:10 (NASB)

Whom have You placed in my life as an
example of Christlike humility?

Year: _____

_____

_____

_____

_____

Year: _____

_____

_____

_____

_____

Year: _____

_____

_____

_____

_____

July 4

The Lord is the Spirit, and where the Spirit of the
Lord is, there is freedom.
—2 Corinthians 3:17 (NCV)

What does it feel like to live free in You?

Year: _____

_____

_____

_____

_____

Year: _____

_____

_____

_____

_____

Year: _____

_____

_____

_____

_____

July 5

If your enemy is hungry, give him food to eat;
if he is thirsty, give him water to drink.
—**Proverbs 25:21 (NIV)**

How can I treat someone who could be seen
as an enemy as a child of Yours?

Year: _____

_____

_____

_____

_____

Year: _____

_____

_____

_____

_____

Year: _____

_____

_____

_____

_____

July 6

*Sing to the L*ORD *a new song,*
for he has done marvelous things...
—Psalm 98:1a (NIV)

What lyrics to a hymn or song make
me feel close to You?

Year: _____

_____
_____
_____
_____

Year: _____

_____
_____
_____
_____

Year: _____

_____
_____
_____
_____

July 7

*Stay alert and be persistent in your prayers
for all believers everywhere.*
—Ephesians 6:18b (NLT)

Who is physically far away but close
to my heart in prayer?

Year: _____

_____

_____

_____

_____

Year: _____

_____

_____

_____

_____

Year: _____

_____

_____

_____

_____

July 8

For God alone, O my soul, wait in silence,
for my hope is from him.
—Psalm 62:5 (ESV)

How hard is it for me to be still
and listen to You?

Year: _____

_____
_____
_____
_____

Year: _____

_____
_____
_____
_____

Year: _____

_____
_____
_____
_____

July 9

"We have no power against this large army that is attacking us.
We don't know what to do, so we look to you for help."
—2 Chronicles 20:12b (NCV)

When have I felt like I was under
attack? Did I turn to You?

Year: _____

_____
_____
_____
_____

Year: _____

_____
_____
_____
_____

Year: _____

_____
_____
_____
_____

July 10

So now there is no condemnation for those
who belong to Christ Jesus.
—Romans 8:1 (NLT)

What have You forgiven me for that I can't
seem to forgive myself for?

Year: _____

_____

_____

_____

_____

Year: _____

_____

_____

_____

_____

Year: _____

_____

_____

_____

_____

July 11

But we have this treasure in jars of clay, to show that the surpassing power belongs to God and not to us.
—2 Corinthians 4:7 (ESV)

What imperfect people resonate with me as examples of power only through faith in You?

Year: _____

_____

_____

_____

_____

Year: _____

_____

_____

_____

_____

Year: _____

_____

_____

_____

_____

July 12

*Your Father knows what you need
before you ask Him.*
—Matthew 6:8b (NASB)

When is one time I have been especially grateful that
You knew what I needed before I did?

Year: _____

_____

_____

_____

_____

Year: _____

_____

_____

_____

_____

Year: _____

_____

_____

_____

_____

July 13

So we, who are many, are one body in Christ,
and individually parts of one another.
—Romans 12:5 (NASB)

What do I appreciate most about the faith
community You have given me?

Year: _____

_____

_____

_____

_____

Year: _____

_____

_____

_____

_____

Year: _____

_____

_____

_____

_____

July 14

Consider it all joy, my brothers and sisters,
when you encounter various trials, knowing that the
testing of your faith produces endurance.
—James 1:2–3 (NASB)

In what struggle do I perceive You teaching me?

Year: _____

_____
_____
_____
_____

Year: _____

_____
_____
_____
_____

Year: _____

_____
_____
_____
_____

July 15

He makes me like a deer that does not stumble
so I can walk on the steep mountains.
—Habakkuk 3:19b (NCV)

What helps me feel strong in my faith?

Year: _____

_____
_____
_____
_____

Year: _____

_____
_____
_____
_____

Year: _____

_____
_____
_____
_____

July 16

Being with you will fill me with joy;
at your right hand I will find pleasure forever.
—Psalm 16:11b (NCV)

What brings me momentary happiness right now,
and what will bring me eternal joy?

Year: _____

_____

_____

_____

_____

Year: _____

_____

_____

_____

_____

Year: _____

_____

_____

_____

_____

July 17

When you walk through fire, you will not be burned,
nor will the flames hurt you.

—Isaiah 43:2b (NCV)

What fire(s) am I facing this week?

Year: _____

_____
_____
_____
_____

Year: _____

_____
_____
_____
_____

Year: _____

_____
_____
_____
_____

July 18

Jesus wept.
—John 11:35 (NKJV)

When was the last time I wept and allowed
You to wipe my tears?

Year: _____

_____
_____
_____
_____

Year: _____

_____
_____
_____
_____

Year: _____

_____
_____
_____

July 19

*I cried aloud to the LORD,
and he answered me from his holy hill.* Selah
—Psalm 3:4 (ESV)

What psalm of my own can I
offer You today?

Year: _____

_____

_____

_____

_____

Year: _____

_____

_____

_____

_____

Year: _____

_____

_____

_____

_____

July 20

*The LORD is near to the brokenhearted
and saves the crushed in spirit.*
—Psalm 34:18 (ESV)

What breaks my heart in this world,
and how can I lift it up to You?

Year: _____

_____
_____
_____
_____

Year: _____

_____
_____
_____
_____

Year: _____

_____
_____
_____
_____

July 21

*Owe no one anything, except to love each other, for the
one who loves another has fulfilled the law.*
—Romans 13:8 (ESV)

Whom do I need to let off the hook?

Year: _____

_____

_____

_____

_____

Year: _____

_____

_____

_____

_____

Year: _____

_____

_____

_____

_____

July 22

If you need wisdom, ask our generous God, and he will give it to you. He will not rebuke you for asking.
—James 1:5 (NLT)

What don't I need to be afraid
to ask You right now?

Year: _____

_____

_____

_____

_____

Year: _____

_____

_____

_____

_____

Year: _____

_____

_____

_____

_____

July 23

A friend loves you all the time,
and a brother helps in time of trouble.
—**Proverbs 17:17 (NCV)**

When is it hard for me to love?

Year: _____

Year: _____

Year: _____

July 24

Immediately the father cried out, "I do believe!
Help me to believe more!"
—Mark 9:24 (NCV)

What do I have too little of in my life?

Year: _____

_____

_____

_____

_____

Year: _____

_____

_____

_____

_____

Year: _____

_____

_____

_____

_____

July 25

Then Jesus said to them, "Be careful and guard against all kinds of greed. Life is not measured by how much one owns."
—Luke 12:15 (NCV)

What do I have too much of in my life?

Year: _____

_____

_____

_____

_____

Year: _____

_____

_____

_____

_____

Year: _____

_____

_____

_____

July 26

When a believing person prays,
great things happen.
—James 5:16b (NCV)

How can You help me overcome any feeling
that my prayer is not effective?

Year: _____

_____
_____
_____
_____

Year: _____

_____
_____
_____
_____

Year: _____

_____
_____
_____
_____

July 27

Tell me in the morning about your love,
because I trust you.
—Psalm 143:8a (NCV)

How can I wake up full of energy to do Your will?

Year: _____

_____

_____

_____

_____

Year: _____

_____

_____

_____

_____

Year: _____

_____

_____

_____

_____

July 28

Turn away from evil and do good;
seek peace and pursue it.
—Psalm 34:14 (ESV)

Who are You nudging me to
reach out to today?

Year: _____

_____
_____
_____
_____

Year: _____

_____
_____
_____
_____

Year: _____

_____
_____
_____
_____

July 29

*I fed you with milk, not solid food, for you
were not ready for it.*

—1 Corinthians 3:2a (ESV)

❧

What did I once believe that I can
chuckle at now?

Year: _____

_____

_____

_____

_____

Year: _____

_____

_____

_____

_____

Year: _____

_____

_____

_____

_____

July 30

What then shall we say to these things?
If God is for us, who can be against us?
—Romans 8:31 (ESV)

When have I felt like the world was against me?
How accurate was my assessment?

Year: _____

_____

_____

_____

_____

Year: _____

_____

_____

_____

_____

Year: _____

_____

_____

_____

_____

July 31

Let not your hearts be troubled,
neither let them be afraid.
—John 14:27b (ESV)

What does my physical body feel like when
I am calm and assured in You?

Year: _____

_____
_____
_____
_____

Year: _____

_____
_____
_____
_____

Year: _____

_____
_____
_____
_____

August 1

Confess your sins to each other and pray for each other so God can heal you.
—James 5:16a (NCV)

Whom do I owe an apology?

Year: _____

_____
_____
_____
_____

Year: _____

_____
_____
_____
_____

Year: _____

_____
_____
_____
_____

August 2

A gentle answer turns away wrath,
but a harsh word stirs up anger.
—**Proverbs 15:1 (NIV)**

Where do I need to show more gentleness?

Year: _____

_____
_____
_____
_____

Year: _____

_____
_____
_____
_____

Year: _____

_____
_____
_____
_____

August 3

All things were made through him, and without him was not any thing made that was made.
—John 1:3 (ESV)

Where in Your creation am I moved to awe?

Year: _____

_____

_____

_____

_____

Year: _____

_____

_____

_____

_____

Year: _____

_____

_____

_____

_____

August 4

The L<small>ORD</small>'s curse is on the house of the wicked,
but he blesses the home of the righteous.
—Proverbs 3:33 (NIV)

❧❧❧

Why have You placed me where I live?

Year: _____

_____

_____

_____

_____

Year: _____

_____

_____

_____

_____

Year: _____

_____

_____

_____

_____

August 5

Do not be overcome by evil, but overcome evil with good.
—Romans 12:21 (NIV)

For what do I need closure in my life?
How can I move forward?

Year: _____

_____

_____

_____

_____

Year: _____

_____

_____

_____

_____

Year: _____

_____

_____

_____

_____

August 6

*No, in all these things we are more than
victorious through him who loved us.*
—Romans 8:37 (NRSVUE)

What kind of "winning" no longer matters
to me because of Jesus's victory?

Year: _____

_____
_____
_____
_____

Year: _____

_____
_____
_____
_____

Year: _____

_____
_____
_____
_____

August 7

*"Whoever has two tunics is to share with him who has none,
and whoever has food is to do likewise."*
—Luke 3:11 (ESV)

What can I share with someone in need?

Year: _____

_____

_____

_____

_____

Year: _____

_____

_____

_____

_____

Year: _____

_____

_____

_____

_____

August 8

According to the grace of God given to me, like a skilled master builder I laid a foundation, and someone else is building upon it.

—1 Corinthians 3:10a (ESV)

Where do I need to put pride aside for
Your greater purpose?

Year: _____

_____

_____

_____

_____

Year: _____

_____

_____

_____

_____

Year: _____

_____

_____

_____

_____

August 9

For everyone has sinned; we all fall short of
God's glorious standard.
—Romans 3:23 (NLT)

In what situation am I setting expectations
for myself too high?

Year: _____

_____
_____
_____

Year: _____

_____
_____
_____

Year: _____

_____
_____
_____

August 10

"But love your enemies, do good to them, and lend to them without expecting to get anything back."
—Luke 6:35a (NIV)

In what situation am I setting expectations
for others too high?

Year: _____

_____
_____
_____
_____

Year: _____

_____
_____
_____
_____

Year: _____

_____
_____
_____
_____

August 11

Yet you know me, LORD;
you see me and test my thoughts about you.
—Jeremiah 12:3a (NIV)

How do I think You see me?

Year: _____

_____

_____

_____

_____

Year: _____

_____

_____

_____

_____

Year: _____

_____

_____

_____

_____

August 12

"Do not fear, for I have redeemed you;
I have summoned you by name; you are mine."
—Isaiah 43:1b (NIV)

How does it feel to be Yours in
this (and every) moment?

Year: _____

_____

_____

_____

_____

Year: _____

_____

_____

_____

_____

Year: _____

_____

_____

_____

_____

August 13

Try to learn what pleases the Lord.
—Ephesians 5:10 (NCV)

What am I trying to take on
that isn't from You?

Year: _____

_____

_____

_____

_____

Year: _____

_____

_____

_____

_____

Year: _____

_____

_____

_____

_____

August 14

Where there is no guidance, a people falls,
but in an abundance of counselors there is safety.
—Proverbs 11:14 (ESV)

Where are You calling me to take
on a leadership role?

Year: _____

_____
_____
_____
_____

Year: _____

_____
_____
_____
_____

Year: _____

_____
_____
_____
_____

August 15

We have peace with God because of what
Jesus Christ our Lord has done for us.

—Romans 5:1b (NLT)

Who needs me to guide them
into Your peace?

Year: _____

_____

_____

_____

_____

Year: _____

_____

_____

_____

_____

Year: _____

_____

_____

_____

_____

August 16

Let your light shine before others, so that they may see your good works and give glory to your Father who is in heaven.
—Matthew 5:16 (ESV)

In what way am I uniquely qualified
to meet a need this week?

Year: _____

_____

_____

_____

_____

Year: _____

_____

_____

_____

_____

Year: _____

_____

_____

_____

_____

August 17

*So let us stop going over the basic teachings
about Christ again and again. Let us go on instead and
become mature in our understanding.*

—Hebrews 6:1a (NLT)

What is the next step in my spiritual growth?

Year: _____

_____

_____

_____

_____

Year: _____

_____

_____

_____

_____

Year: _____

_____

_____

_____

_____

August 18

He made us, and we are his.
We are his people, the sheep of his pasture.
—Psalm 100:3b (NLT)

What do I understand about myself from
what I know about You?

Year: _____

_____
_____
_____
_____

Year: _____

_____
_____
_____
_____

Year: _____

_____
_____
_____
_____

August 19

*If anyone, then, knows the good they ought to do
and doesn't do it, it is sin for them.*

—James 4:17 (NIV)

What calling do I need to stop avoiding?

Year: _____

_____

_____

_____

_____

Year: _____

_____

_____

_____

_____

Year: _____

_____

_____

_____

_____

August 20

He is the faithful God, keeping his covenant of love to a thousand generations of those who love him and keep his commandments.
—Deuteronomy 7:9b (NIV)

What recent changes in my life has Your constancy brought me through?

Year: _____

_____

_____

_____

_____

Year: _____

_____

_____

_____

_____

Year: _____

_____

_____

_____

_____

August 21

Seek the LORD and his strength;
seek his presence continually!
—1 Chronicles 16:11 (ESV)

How can I include You in more
of my daily rituals?

Year: _____

_____
_____
_____
_____

Year: _____

_____
_____
_____
_____

Year: _____

_____
_____
_____
_____

August 22

*Open my eyes to see
the wonderful truths in your instructions.*
—Psalm 119:18 (NLT)

What do I need clarity on
from You right now?

Year: _____

_____

_____

_____

_____

Year: _____

_____

_____

_____

_____

Year: _____

_____

_____

_____

_____

August 23

Great is our Lord, and abundant in power;
his understanding is beyond measure.
—Psalm 147:5 (ESV)

What picture or work of art brings to mind how
You are working in my life?

Year: _____

_____
_____
_____
_____

Year: _____

_____
_____
_____
_____

Year: _____

_____
_____
_____
_____

August 24

*"You are the light of the world. A city that is
set on a hill cannot be hidden."*
—Matthew 5:14 (NKJV)

How can I shine my light brighter
and farther for You?

Year: _____

_____
_____
_____
_____

Year: _____

_____
_____
_____
_____

Year: _____

_____
_____
_____
_____

August 25

One who is slow to anger is better than the mighty,
and one whose temper is controlled than one who captures a city.
—Proverbs 16:32 (NRSVUE)

What tempts my temper? How can I
better control my response?

Year: _____

_____
_____
_____
_____

Year: _____

_____
_____
_____
_____

Year: _____

_____
_____
_____
_____

August 26

*And this is love, that we walk according
to his commandments...*
—2 John 1:6a (NRSVUE)

In what area of my life do I need to
work on obedience to You?

Year: _____

_____

_____

_____

_____

Year: _____

_____

_____

_____

_____

Year: _____

_____

_____

_____

August 27

But the people who trust the LORD will become strong again.
They will rise up as an eagle in the sky. . .
—Isaiah 40:31a (NCV)

How do my energy levels change when
I pause to connect with You?

Year: _____

_____

_____

_____

_____

Year: _____

_____

_____

_____

_____

Year: _____

_____

_____

_____

_____

August 28

Therefore, accept each other just as Christ has accepted you so that God will be given glory.
—Romans 15:7 (NLT)

When have I struggled to
accept other people?

Year: _____

_____

_____

_____

_____

Year: _____

_____

_____

_____

_____

Year: _____

_____

_____

_____

_____

August 29

"Now you Pharisees clean the outside of the cup and of the dish, but inside you are full of greed and wickedness."
—Luke 11:39b (NRSVUE)

What do I get hung up on that
doesn't matter to You?

Year: _____

_____
_____
_____
_____

Year: _____

_____
_____
_____
_____

Year: _____

_____
_____
_____

August 30

So we are Christ's ambassadors; God is making his appeal through us. We speak for Christ when we plead, "Come back to God!"
—2 Corinthians 5:20 (NLT)

How can I be a good ambassador for
Christ this week?

Year: _____

_____
_____
_____
_____

Year: _____

_____
_____
_____
_____

Year: _____

_____
_____
_____
_____

August 31

"The LORD himself will fight for you.
Just stay calm."
—Exodus 14:14 (NLT)

In what situation do I need to simply
trust that I am in Your hands?

Year: _____

_____
_____
_____
_____

Year: _____

_____
_____
_____
_____

Year: _____

_____
_____
_____
_____

September 1

O LORD my God, I cried to you for help,
and you have healed me.

—Psalm 30:2 (ESV)

How have I recently experienced Your healing?

Year: _____

_____
_____
_____
_____

Year: _____

_____
_____
_____
_____

Year: _____

_____
_____
_____
_____

September 2

Many are the sorrows of the wicked,
but steadfast love surrounds the one who trusts in the LORD.
—Psalm 32:10 (ESV)

Where do I feel Your steadfast love?

Year: _____

_____
_____
_____
_____

Year: _____

_____
_____
_____
_____

Year: _____

_____
_____
_____

September 3

"Do not judge, and you will not be judged."
—Luke 6:37a (NIV)

When have I struggled to not judge others?
What helps me withhold judgment?

Year: _____

_____
_____
_____
_____

Year: _____

_____
_____
_____
_____

Year: _____

_____
_____
_____

September 4

It is not that we think we are qualified to do anything on our own. Our qualification comes from God.
—2 Corinthians 3:5 (NLT)

In what area of my life are You telling me that
I am enough through Your power?

Year: _____

_____

_____

_____

_____

Year: _____

_____

_____

_____

_____

Year: _____

_____

_____

_____

_____

September 5

This hope is a strong and trustworthy anchor for our souls. It leads us through the curtain into God's inner sanctuary.
—Hebrews 6:19 (NLT)

How could remembering to hold Your hope
as an anchor change my day?

Year: _____

_____
_____
_____
_____

Year: _____

_____
_____
_____
_____

Year: _____

_____
_____
_____
_____

September 6

Blessed are those who dwell in your house;
they are ever praising you.
—Psalm 84:4 (NIV)

What simple blessings fill me
with praise right now?

Year: _____

_____
_____
_____
_____

Year: _____

_____
_____
_____
_____

Year: _____

_____
_____
_____
_____

September 7

But we are citizens of heaven, where the Lord Jesus Christ lives.
And we are eagerly waiting for him to return as our Savior.
—Philippians 3:20 (NLT)

How am I living my life differently knowing
that my true citizenship is in heaven?

Year: _____

_____
_____
_____
_____

Year: _____

_____
_____
_____
_____

Year: _____

_____
_____
_____

September 8

The tongue can bring death or life;
those who love to talk will reap the consequences.
—Proverbs 18:21 (NLT)

How have my words helped or hurt me recently?

Year: _____

_____
_____
_____
_____

Year: _____

_____
_____
_____
_____

Year: _____

_____
_____
_____
_____

September 9

Jesus said, "If you hold to my teaching, you are really my disciples.
Then you will know the truth, and the truth will set you free."
—John 8:31b–32 (NIV)

What "truth" is someone trying to convince me
to believe that isn't Your truth?

Year: _____

_____

_____

_____

_____

Year: _____

_____

_____

_____

_____

Year: _____

_____

_____

_____

_____

September 10

The world and its desires pass away, but whoever does the will of God lives forever.

—1 John 2:17 (NIV)

How can I guard my peace from
the noise of the world?

Year: _____

_____

_____

_____

_____

Year: _____

_____

_____

_____

_____

Year: _____

_____

_____

_____

_____

September 11

Bear with each other and forgive one another if any of you has a grievance against someone. Forgive as the Lord forgave you.
—Colossians 3:13 (NIV)

In what situation do I need to forgive
without further delay?

Year: _____

_____

_____

_____

_____

Year: _____

_____

_____

_____

_____

Year: _____

_____

_____

_____

_____

September 12

*I have learned the secret of being content
in any and every situation, whether well fed or hungry,
whether living in plenty or in want.*
—Philippians 4:12b (NIV)

What do I need to put aside to
be content right now?

Year: _____

Year: _____

Year: _____

September 13

*After this prayer, the meeting place shook,
and they were all filled with the Holy Spirit. Then they
preached the word of God with boldness.*

—Acts 4:31 (NLT)

In what situation could You
fill me with boldness?

Year: _____

_____

_____

_____

_____

Year: _____

_____

_____

_____

_____

Year: _____

_____

_____

_____

_____

September 14

Anyone who claims to be in the light but hates
a brother or sister is still in the darkness.
—1 John 2:9 (NIV)

Who pushes my buttons that I need to
address in a more loving way?

Year: _____

_____
_____
_____
_____

Year: _____

_____
_____
_____
_____

Year: _____

_____
_____
_____
_____

September 15

*You keep him in perfect peace
whose mind is stayed on you. . .*
—Isaiah 26:3a (ESV)

How can I settle my mind when
I feel overwhelmed?

Year: _____

_____
_____
_____
_____

Year: _____

_____
_____
_____
_____

Year: _____

_____
_____
_____
_____

September 16

I have stored up your word in my heart,
that I might not sin against you.
—Psalm 119:11 (ESV)

What temptation am I struggling with that
Your word can help me overcome?

Year: _____

_____

_____

_____

_____

Year: _____

_____

_____

_____

_____

Year: _____

_____

_____

_____

_____

September 17

When the cares of my heart are many,
your consolations cheer my soul.
—Psalm 94:19 (ESV)

What anxiety do I need to release
to You right now?

Year: _____

_____
_____
_____
_____

Year: _____

_____
_____
_____
_____

Year: _____

_____
_____
_____
_____

September 18

But the word of God cannot be chained.
—2 Timothy 2:9b (NLT)

What would my day be like if I let
Your word reign?

Year: _____

_____

_____

_____

_____

Year: _____

_____

_____

_____

_____

Year: _____

_____

_____

_____

_____

September 19

*So give yourselves completely to God. Stand against
the devil, and the devil will run from you.*

—James 4:7 (NCV)

When have I felt the strongest attack from
the enemy in the past year?

Year: _____

_____
_____
_____
_____

Year: _____

_____
_____
_____
_____

Year: _____

_____
_____
_____
_____

September 20

*"O Sovereign LORD! You made the heavens and earth by your
strong hand and powerful arm. Nothing is too hard for you!"*
—Jeremiah 32:17 (NLT)

What opportunities for enjoying Creation
are You placing in my life?

Year: _____

_____
_____
_____
_____

Year: _____

_____
_____
_____
_____

Year: _____

_____
_____
_____
_____

September 21

Look carefully then how you walk, not as unwise but as wise, making the best use of the time, because the days are evil.
—Ephesians 5:15–16 (ESV)

How can I honor You better
with my time?

Year: _____

_____
_____
_____
_____

Year: _____

_____
_____
_____
_____

Year: _____

_____
_____
_____
_____

September 22

"'We had to celebrate this happy day. For your brother was dead and has come back to life! He was lost, but now he is found!'"
—Luke 15:32 (NLT)

What unexpected gift from You
can I celebrate?

Year: _____

_____

_____

_____

_____

Year: _____

_____

_____

_____

_____

Year: _____

_____

_____

_____

_____

September 23

*"God is spirit, and those who worship him must
worship in spirit and truth."*
—John 4:24 (ESV)

How can I allow the Spirit to more
fully enter my worship?

Year: _____

_____
_____
_____
_____

Year: _____

_____
_____
_____
_____

Year: _____

_____
_____
_____
_____

September 24

*I sought the LORD, and he answered me
and delivered me from all my fears.*
—Psalm 34:4 (ESV)

What is one fear from which You
have delivered me?

Year: _____

_____
_____
_____
_____

Year: _____

_____
_____
_____
_____

Year: _____

_____
_____
_____
_____

September 25

If you are trying hard to do good, no one can really hurt you.
But even if you suffer for doing right, you are blessed.
—1 Peter 3:13–14 (NCV)

When did doing the right thing feel risky
but You kept me safe?

Year: _____

_____
_____
_____
_____

Year: _____

_____
_____
_____
_____

Year: _____

_____
_____
_____
_____

September 26

Above all else, guard your heart,
for everything you do flows from it.
—Proverbs 4:23 (NIV)

How can I guard my heart today?

Year: _____

_____

_____

_____

_____

Year: _____

_____

_____

_____

_____

Year: _____

_____

_____

_____

_____

September 27

Jesus said to him, "'You shall love the LORD your God with all your heart, with all your soul, and with all your mind.'"
—Matthew 22:37 (NKJV)

Where do I need to be more
"all in" for You?

Year: _____

_____

_____

_____

_____

Year: _____

_____

_____

_____

_____

Year: _____

_____

_____

_____

_____

September 28

Your lives are a letter written in our hearts; everyone can read it and recognize our good work among you.
—2 Corinthians 3:2b (NLT)

To whom can I write a letter to encourage their faith?

Year: _____

_____
_____
_____
_____

Year: _____

_____
_____
_____
_____

Year: _____

_____
_____
_____

September 29

*Pursue righteousness and a godly life, along with
faith, love, perseverance, and gentleness.*
—1 Timothy 6:11b (NLT)

How would my family and friends
describe my faith?

Year: _____

_____

_____

_____

_____

Year: _____

_____

_____

_____

_____

Year: _____

_____

_____

_____

_____

September 30

*The life I now live in the flesh I live by faith in the
Son of God, who loved me and gave himself for me.*
—Galatians 2:20b (ESV)

How do I describe my faith?

Year: _____

_____

_____

_____

_____

Year: _____

_____

_____

_____

_____

Year: _____

_____

_____

_____

_____

October 1

Wait for the LORD;
be strong, and let your heart take courage. . .
—Psalm 27:14a (ESV)

When do I need to slow down and
not rush Your timing?

Year: _____

_____

_____

_____

_____

Year: _____

_____

_____

_____

_____

Year: _____

_____

_____

_____

_____

October 2

Do not pronounce judgment . . . before the Lord comes,
who will bring to light the things now hidden in darkness. . .
—1 Corinthians 4:5a (ESV)

What situation do I need to trust God will resolve
in His time and in His way?

Year: _____

_____
_____
_____
_____

Year: _____

_____
_____
_____
_____

Year: _____

_____
_____
_____
_____

October 3

"A new commandment I give to you, that you love one another:
just as I have loved you, you also are to love one another."
—John 13:34 (ESV)

When do I overcomplicate love?

Year: _____

_____
_____
_____
_____

Year: _____

_____
_____
_____
_____

Year: _____

_____
_____
_____
_____

October 4

"Take my yoke upon you, and learn from me, for I am gentle and lowly in heart, and you will find rest for your souls."
—Matthew 11:29 (ESV)

What does my soul need rest from right now?

Year: _____

_____
_____
_____
_____

Year: _____

_____
_____
_____
_____

Year: _____

_____
_____
_____
_____

October 5

*Before daybreak the next morning, Jesus got up
and went out to an isolated place to pray.*
—Mark 1:35 (NLT)

How can I strengthen my prayer life?

Year: _____

_____

_____

_____

_____

Year: _____

_____

_____

_____

_____

Year: _____

_____

_____

_____

_____

October 6

*"Do not be anxious about your life, what you will eat,
nor about your body, what you will put on."*
—Luke 12:22b (ESV)

What worldly concerns do I give too much focus?

Year: _____

_____

_____

_____

_____

Year: _____

_____

_____

_____

_____

Year: _____

_____

_____

_____

_____

October 7

*"The mountains and the hills before you
shall break forth into singing. . ."*
—Isaiah 55:12b (ESV)

Where have I found Your joy this week?

Year: _____

_____

_____

_____

_____

Year: _____

_____

_____

_____

_____

Year: _____

_____

_____

_____

_____

October 8

For we walk by faith, not by sight.
—2 Corinthians 5:7 (NKJV)

In what area of my daily faith walk am I still
at least a little uncomfortable?

Year: _____

_____

_____

_____

_____

Year: _____

_____

_____

_____

_____

Year: _____

_____

_____

_____

_____

October 9

The LORD directs our steps,
so why try to understand everything along the way?
—Proverbs 20:24 (NLT)

What do I need to just do and
not try to analyze?

Year: _____

_____

_____

_____

_____

Year: _____

_____

_____

_____

_____

Year: _____

_____

_____

_____

_____

October 10

*God saved you by his grace when you believed. And you can't
take credit for this; it is a gift from God.*
—Ephesians 2:8 (NLT)

How has Your grace changed me?

Year: _____

_____
_____
_____
_____

Year: _____

_____
_____
_____
_____

Year: _____

_____
_____
_____
_____

October 11

Great is his faithfulness;
his mercies begin afresh each morning.
—Lamentations 3:23 (NLT)

What do I need to remind myself each morning?

Year: _____

_____
_____
_____
_____

Year: _____

_____
_____
_____
_____

Year: _____

_____
_____
_____
_____

October 12

Ascribe to the LORD the glory due his name;
bring an offering and come into his courts.
—Psalm 96:8 (NIV)

What offering can I bring You today?

Year: _____

_____
_____
_____
_____

Year: _____

_____
_____
_____
_____

Year: _____

_____
_____
_____
_____

October 13

I will give them a crown to replace their ashes,
and the oil of gladness to replace their sorrow...
—Isaiah 61:3b (NCV)

Where have You brought about beauty
from ashes in my life?

Year: _____

Year: _____

Year: _____

October *14*

It is painful at the time, but later, after we have learned from it,
we have peace, because we start living in the right way.
—Hebrews 12:11b (NCV)

What difficult time did I go through that
I now realize helped me grow?

Year: _____

_____
_____
_____
_____

Year: _____

_____
_____
_____
_____

Year: _____

_____
_____
_____
_____

October 15

*In the past you were full of darkness, but now you are full of
light in the Lord. So live like children who belong to the light.*
—Ephesians 5:8 (NCV)

How can I be a light for the lost?

Year: _____

_____
_____
_____
_____

Year: _____

_____
_____
_____
_____

Year: _____

_____
_____
_____
_____

October *16*

Jesus looked at them and said, "With man this is impossible,
but with God all things are possible."
—Matthew 19:26 (NIV)

When am I tempted to put limits on You?

Year: _____

_____
_____
_____
_____

Year: _____

_____
_____
_____
_____

Year: _____

_____
_____
_____
_____

October 17

Just as a body, though one, has many parts, but all its many parts form one body, so it is with Christ.
—1 Corinthians 12:12 (NIV)

How can I support others' gifts
in Kingdom work?

Year: _____

_____
_____
_____
_____

Year: _____

_____
_____
_____
_____

Year: _____

_____
_____
_____
_____

October 18

Unless the LORD builds the house,
the builders labor in vain.
—Psalm 127:1a (NIV)

When have I trusted You completely?

Year: _____

_____

_____

_____

_____

Year: _____

_____

_____

_____

_____

Year: _____

_____

_____

_____

_____

October 19

If we are faithless, He remains faithful,
for He cannot deny Himself.
—2 Timothy 2:13 (NASB)

What truths can I hold fast to even
when doubts pop up?

Year: _____

_____

_____

_____

_____

Year: _____

_____

_____

_____

_____

Year: _____

_____

_____

_____

_____

October 20

*There will be more joy in heaven over one sinner who repents
than over ninety-nine righteous persons who need no repentance.*
—Luke 15:7 (NRSVUE)

What do I need to confess to You?

Year: _____

_____

_____

_____

_____

Year: _____

_____

_____

_____

_____

Year: _____

_____

_____

_____

_____

October 21

*"Blessed are the merciful, for they
will receive mercy."*
—Matthew 5:7 (NRSVUE)

∽✓✑

When have I shown mercy?

Year: _____

_____
_____
_____
_____

Year: _____

_____
_____
_____
_____

Year: _____

_____
_____
_____
_____

October 22

Worship the LORD in the splendor of his holiness;
tremble before him, all the earth.
—Psalm 96:9 (NIV)

What recent experience has brought me
to my knees before You?

Year: _____

_____

_____

_____

_____

Year: _____

_____

_____

_____

_____

Year: _____

_____

_____

_____

_____

October 23

*"Greater love has no one than this: to lay down
one's life for one's friends."*
—John 15:13 (NIV)

How can I show Your love
to my friends?

Year: _____

_____

_____

_____

_____

Year: _____

_____

_____

_____

_____

Year: _____

_____

_____

_____

_____

October 24

Let everything that has breath praise the LORD.
—Psalm 150:6a (NKJV)

What praise can I give You for
simply who You are?

Year: _____

_____

_____

_____

_____

Year: _____

_____

_____

_____

_____

Year: _____

_____

_____

_____

_____

October 25

And God saw everything that he had made,
and behold, it was very good.
—Genesis 1:31a (ESV)

When do I need to remind myself that I am
good because I am Yours?

Year: _____

_____

_____

_____

_____

Year: _____

_____

_____

_____

_____

Year: _____

_____

_____

_____

_____

October 26

But as for me, it is good to be near God.
—Psalm 73:28a (NIV)

How can I feel even closer
to You right now?

Year: _____

_____
_____
_____
_____

Year: _____

_____
_____
_____
_____

Year: _____

_____
_____
_____
_____

October 27

You were taught to be made new in your hearts, to become a new person . . . made to be like God—made to be truly good and holy.
—Ephesians 4:23–24 (NCV)

Can people tell I am different because
of my faith in You?

Year: _____

_____
_____
_____
_____

Year: _____

_____
_____
_____
_____

Year: _____

_____
_____
_____
_____

October 28

*Let us hold firmly to the hope that we have confessed,
because we can trust God to do what he promised.*
—Hebrews 10:23 (NCV)

What positive habits support my faith?

Year: _____

_____

_____

_____

_____

Year: _____

_____

_____

_____

_____

Year: _____

_____

_____

_____

_____

October 29

Pride goes before destruction,
and haughtiness before a fall.
—**Proverbs 16:18 (NLT)**

When does my pride threaten to
pull me away from You?

Year: _____

_____
_____
_____
_____

Year: _____

_____
_____
_____
_____

Year: _____

_____
_____
_____
_____

October 30

No eye has seen any God besides you,
who acts on behalf of those who wait for him.
—Isaiah 64:4b (NIV)

What can still surprise me about You?

Year: _____

_____

_____

_____

_____

Year: _____

_____

_____

_____

_____

Year: _____

_____

_____

_____

_____

October 31

When I am afraid, I put my trust in you.
What can mere mortals do to me?
—Psalm 56:3, 4c (NIV)

What fear am I trying to handle on my own
instead of bringing it to You?

Year: _____

_____

_____

_____

_____

Year: _____

_____

_____

_____

_____

Year: _____

_____

_____

_____

_____

November 1

For the sake of Christ...I am content with weaknesses, insults, hardships, persecutions, and calamities. For when I am weak, then I am strong.

—2 Corinthians 12:10 (ESV)

When have I run rather than
face something hard?

Year: _____

_____

_____

_____

_____

Year: _____

_____

_____

_____

_____

Year: _____

_____

_____

_____

_____

November 2

And what does the LORD require of you?
To act justly and to love mercy and to walk humbly with your God.
—Micah 6:8b (NIV)

How can I live justly, mercifully,
and humbly for You today?

Year: _____

_____
_____
_____
_____

Year: _____

_____
_____
_____
_____

Year: _____

_____
_____
_____
_____

November 3

For you created my inmost being;
you knit me together in my mother's womb.
—Psalm 139:13 (NIV)

What do I love most about the way
You have made me?

Year: _____

_____

_____

_____

_____

Year: _____

_____

_____

_____

_____

Year: _____

_____

_____

_____

_____

November 4

So faith by itself, if it has no works, is dead.
—James 2:17 (NRSVUE)

How does my faith make me
want to take action?

Year: _____

_____

_____

_____

_____

Year: _____

_____

_____

_____

_____

Year: _____

_____

_____

_____

_____

November 5

Your word is a lamp to my feet
and a light to my path.
—Psalm 119:105 (NRSVUE)

⸙

When am I tempted to compare faith journeys
instead of focusing on my own path?

Year: _____

_____
_____
_____
_____

Year: _____

_____
_____
_____
_____

Year: _____

_____
_____
_____
_____

November 6

Look, the winter is past;
the rains are over and gone.
—Song of Solomon 2:11 (NCV)

What times of the year do I most struggle?
How can I be on guard?

Year: _____

_____

_____

_____

_____

Year: _____

_____

_____

_____

_____

Year: _____

_____

_____

_____

_____

November 7

So encourage each other and build each other up,
just as you are already doing.
—1 Thessalonians 5:11 (NLT)

How can I encourage someone I sense
is losing their faith?

Year: _____

_____
_____
_____
_____

Year: _____

_____
_____
_____
_____

Year: _____

_____
_____
_____
_____

November 8

"You are worried and upset over all these details! There is only one thing worth being concerned about."
—Luke 10:41b–42a (NLT)

What is the biggest distraction from
You in my life right now?

Year: _____

_____
_____
_____
_____

Year: _____

_____
_____
_____
_____

Year: _____

_____
_____
_____
_____

November 9

"Yes, I am the vine; you are the branches. Those who remain in me, and I in them, will produce much fruit."
—John 15:5a (NLT)

What experience has helped my faith
branch out the most this year?

Year: _____

_____

_____

_____

_____

Year: _____

_____

_____

_____

_____

Year: _____

_____

_____

_____

_____

November 10

If we confess our sins, he who is faithful and just will forgive us our sins and cleanse us from all unrighteousness.
—1 John 1:9 (NRSVUE)

What source of guilt threatens
to hold me back?

Year: _____

_____

_____

_____

_____

Year: _____

_____

_____

_____

_____

Year: _____

_____

_____

_____

_____

November 11

*Do you not know that you are God's temple and
that God's Spirit dwells in you?*
—1 Corinthians 3:16 (NRSVUE)

How do I show care for myself as Your beloved
child in whom the Spirit dwells?

Year: _____

_____

_____

_____

_____

Year: _____

_____

_____

_____

_____

Year: _____

_____

_____

_____

_____

November 12

Do not be misled: "Bad company corrupts good character."
—1 Corinthians 15:33 (NIV)

Are my relationships helping or
hindering my faith?

Year: _____

_____
_____
_____
_____

Year: _____

_____
_____
_____
_____

Year: _____

_____
_____
_____
_____

November 13

And this is eternal life: that people know you, the only true God, and that they know Jesus Christ, the One you sent.
—John 17:3 (NCV)

What feels just right in my
relationship with You?

Year: _____

_____
_____
_____
_____

Year: _____

_____
_____
_____
_____

Year: _____

_____
_____
_____
_____

November 14

Just as the heavens are higher than the earth,
so are my ways higher than your ways. . .
—Isaiah 55:9a (NCV)

What has turned out better when
I turned it over to You?

Year: _____

_____

_____

_____

_____

Year: _____

_____

_____

_____

_____

Year: _____

_____

_____

_____

_____

November 15

*But when you pray, go away by yourself, shut the door
behind you, and pray to your Father in private.*
—Matthew 6:6a (NLT)

Where can I be quiet with You today?

Year: _____

_____
_____
_____
_____

Year: _____

_____
_____
_____
_____

Year: _____

_____
_____
_____
_____

November 16

"I no longer call you servants . . . I have called you friends. . ."
—John 15:15 (NIV)

Whom can I befriend outside my usual circle?

Year: _____

_____

_____

_____

_____

Year: _____

_____

_____

_____

_____

Year: _____

_____

_____

_____

_____

November 17

Though they stumble, they will never fall,
for the LORD holds them by the hand.
—Psalm 37:24 (NLT)

When have You pulled me up again from a stumble?

Year: _____

_____

_____

_____

_____

Year: _____

_____

_____

_____

_____

Year: _____

_____

_____

_____

_____

November 18

He is close to those who trust in him.
—Nahum 1:7b (NLT)

For what loss in my life can You bring comfort?

Year: _____

_____

_____

_____

_____

Year: _____

_____

_____

_____

_____

Year: _____

_____

_____

_____

_____

November 19

O God, you know how foolish I am;
my sins cannot be hidden from you.
—Psalm 69:5 (NLT)

What do I need to let out today that
I feel like I can only tell You?

Year: _____

_____

_____

_____

_____

Year: _____

_____

_____

_____

_____

Year: _____

_____

_____

_____

_____

November 20

The name of the LORD is a strong tower;
the righteous run into it and are safe.
—**Proverbs 18:10 (NRSVUE)**

What name(s) do I feel most comfortable calling You?

Year: _____

_____
_____
_____
_____

Year: _____

_____
_____
_____
_____

Year: _____

_____
_____
_____
_____

November 21

*"My command is this: Love each other
as I have loved you."*
—John 15:12 (NIV)

What places in my community need Your love
to come to them through me?

Year: _____
_____
_____
_____
_____

Year: _____
_____
_____
_____
_____

Year: _____
_____
_____
_____
_____

November 22

*Make it your goal to live a quiet life, minding your own business
and working with your hands, just as we instructed you before.*
—1 Thessalonians 4:11 (NLT)

How can I use my hands to serve You?

Year: _____

_____
_____
_____
_____

Year: _____

_____
_____
_____
_____

Year: _____

_____
_____
_____
_____

November 23

*The righteous flourish like the palm tree
and grow like a cedar in Lebanon.*
—Psalm 92:12 (ESV)

What is one area of my life that is
thriving because of You?

Year: _____

_____

_____

_____

_____

Year: _____

_____

_____

_____

_____

Year: _____

_____

_____

_____

_____

November 24

Let your eyes look straight ahead;
fix your gaze directly before you.
—Proverbs 4:25 (NIV)

In what area of my life do I
need more focus?

Year: _____

_____
_____
_____
_____

Year: _____

_____
_____
_____
_____

Year: _____

_____
_____
_____
_____

November 25

Two are better than one . . .
one can help the other up.
—Ecclesiastes 4:9a, 10b (NIV)

Who has helped me up in Your name?

Year: _____

_____
_____
_____
_____

Year: _____

_____
_____
_____
_____

Year: _____

_____
_____
_____
_____

November 26

*May the God of hope fill you with all joy and peace
as you trust in him, so that you may overflow with
hope by the power of the Holy Spirit.*

—Romans 15:13 (NIV)

When do I feel most hopeful?

Year: _____

_____

_____

_____

_____

Year: _____

_____

_____

_____

_____

Year: _____

_____

_____

_____

_____

November 27

*Jesus stood up and commanded the wind
and said to the waves, "Quiet! Be still!" Then the wind
stopped, and it became completely calm.*

—Mark 4:39 (NCV)

What storm in my life am I praying
for You to calm?

Year: _____

_____

_____

_____

_____

Year: _____

_____

_____

_____

_____

Year: _____

_____

_____

_____

_____

November 28

He guides me along the right paths
for his name's sake.
—Psalm 23:3b (NIV)

Where are You calling me to travel?

Year: _____

_____
_____
_____
_____

Year: _____

_____
_____
_____
_____

Year: _____

_____
_____
_____
_____

November 29

Do not merely listen to the word, and so deceive yourselves. Do what it says.
—James 1:22 (NIV)

What action did I feel You leading me
to take in the past week?

Year: _____

_____

_____

_____

_____

Year: _____

_____

_____

_____

_____

Year: _____

_____

_____

_____

_____

November 30

Let your speech always be gracious, seasoned with salt, so that you may know how you ought to answer each person.
—Colossians 4:6 (ESV)

What words did I feel You leading me
to speak in the past week?

Year: _____

_____

_____

_____

_____

Year: _____

_____

_____

_____

_____

Year: _____

_____

_____

_____

_____

December 1

Work willingly at whatever you do, as though you were working for the Lord rather than for people.
—Colossians 3:23 (NLT)

Is the goal of my work healthy
and faithful to You?

Year: _____

_____
_____
_____
_____

Year: _____

_____
_____
_____
_____

Year: _____

_____
_____
_____
_____

December 2

He gives breath to everyone,
life to everyone who walks the earth.
—Isaiah 42:5b (NLT)

❦

As I breathe deeply, what words
do I hear from You?

Year: _____

_____

_____

_____

_____

Year: _____

_____

_____

_____

_____

Year: _____

_____

_____

_____

_____

December 3

*"For I will satisfy the weary soul, and every
languishing soul I will replenish."*
—Jeremiah 31:25 (ESV)

What gives me satisfaction in any "ordinary" day?

Year: _____

_____
_____
_____
_____

Year: _____

_____
_____
_____
_____

Year: _____

_____
_____
_____
_____

December 4

*They broke bread in their homes and ate together
with glad and sincere hearts. . .*
—Acts 2:46b (NIV)

With whom are You calling me to break bread?

Year: _____

_____

_____

_____

_____

Year: _____

_____

_____

_____

_____

Year: _____

_____

_____

_____

_____

December 5

*Keep putting into practice all you learned and received
from me . . . Then the God of peace will be with you.*
—Philippians 4:9 (NLT)

How can I clear away negative thoughts?

Year: _____

_____
_____
_____
_____

Year: _____

_____
_____
_____
_____

Year: _____

_____
_____
_____
_____

December 6

Moved with compassion, Jesus reached out and touched him. "I am willing," he said. "Be healed!"
—Mark 1:41 (NLT)

In whose touch can I feel Your love?

Year: _____

Year: _____

Year: _____

December 7

And Jacob was left alone. And a man wrestled
with him until the breaking of the day.
—Genesis 32:24 (ESV)

When have You welcomed me to wrestle
with You and be touched?

Year: _____

_____

_____

_____

_____

Year: _____

_____

_____

_____

_____

Year: _____

_____

_____

_____

_____

December 8

"I saw the LORD sitting on His throne, and all the host of heaven standing by, on His right hand and on His left."
—1 Kings 22:19b (NKJV)

How do I picture meeting You
on Your throne?

Year: _____

_____

_____

_____

_____

Year: _____

_____

_____

_____

_____

Year: _____

_____

_____

_____

_____

December 9

So we don't look at the troubles we can see now;
rather, we fix our gaze on things that cannot be seen.
—2 Corinthians 4:18a (NLT)

What do I need to remind myself is temporary?

Year: _____

_____

_____

_____

_____

Year: _____

_____

_____

_____

_____

Year: _____

_____

_____

_____

_____

December 10

Yes, each of us will give a personal account to God.
—Romans 14:12 (NLT)

For whom or what am I not responsible?

Year: _____

_____
_____
_____
_____

Year: _____

_____
_____
_____
_____

Year: _____

_____
_____
_____
_____

December 11

A spiritual gift is given to each of us
so we can help each other.
—1 Corinthians 12:7 (NLT)

What spiritual gift do I have that
someone else needs right now?

Year: _____

_____
_____
_____
_____

Year: _____

_____
_____
_____
_____

Year: _____

_____
_____
_____
_____

December 12

Each of you should give what you have decided in your heart to give, not reluctantly or under compulsion, for God loves a cheerful giver.
—2 Corinthians 9:7 (NIV)

What physical gift do I have that
someone else needs right now?

Year: _____

_____
_____
_____
_____

Year: _____

_____
_____
_____
_____

Year: _____

_____
_____
_____
_____

December 13

"Who are you, Lord?" Saul asked.
—Acts 9:5a (NIV)

Do I truly know who You are and how You are
working right now in my life?

Year: _____

_____

_____

_____

_____

Year: _____

_____

_____

_____

_____

Year: _____

_____

_____

_____

_____

December 14

They received the word with great eagerness, examining the Scriptures daily to see whether these things were so.
—Acts 17:11b (NASB)

How eagerly do I receive and examine Your word?

Year: _____

_____

_____

_____

_____

Year: _____

_____

_____

_____

_____

Year: _____

_____

_____

_____

_____

December 15

*He is your glory and He is your God, who has done these great
and awesome things for you which your eyes have seen.*
—Deuteronomy 10:21 (NASB)

What great and awesome things
have You shown me?

Year: _____

_____

_____

_____

_____

Year: _____

_____

_____

_____

_____

Year: _____

_____

_____

_____

_____

December 16

"Where you go I will go, and where you stay I will stay. Your people will be my people and your God my God."
—Ruth 1:16b (NIV)

What are the biggest commitments in my life right now? Do they align with Your priorities?

Year: _____

_____

_____

_____

_____

Year: _____

_____

_____

_____

_____

Year: _____

_____

_____

_____

_____

December 17

*And David realized that the LORD had appointed him
as king over Israel, and that He had exalted his kingdom
for the sake of His people Israel.*
—2 Samuel 5:12 (NASB)

When have You blessed me so that I could
in turn bless someone else?

Year: _____

_____

_____

_____

_____

Year: _____

_____

_____

_____

_____

Year: _____

_____

_____

_____

_____

December 18

*"Yet who knows whether you have come to the kingdom
for such a time as this?"*
—Esther 4:14b (NKJV)

What place or position have You put
me in to do Your will?

Year: _____

_____
_____
_____
_____

Year: _____

_____
_____
_____
_____

Year: _____

_____
_____
_____
_____

December 19

Hopes placed in mortals die with them;
all the promise of their power comes to nothing.
—Proverbs 11:7 (NIV)

⟡

To whom or where is it tempting to
mistakenly look for power?

Year: _____

_____
_____
_____
_____

Year: _____

_____
_____
_____
_____

Year: _____

_____
_____
_____

December 20

"You will surely wear out...because the task is too heavy for you; you cannot do it alone."
—Exodus 18:18 (NASB)

Where am I trying to take on too much?
Who can I call on for help?

Year: _____

_____
_____
_____
_____

Year: _____

_____
_____
_____
_____

Year: _____

_____
_____
_____
_____

December 21

*In the kingdom of God, eating and drinking
are not important. The important things are living right
with God, peace, and joy in the Holy Spirit.*
—Romans 14:17 (NCV)

Is there anything I'm getting caught up in this season
that is robbing me of true joy?

Year: _____

Year: _____

Year: _____

December 22

*God blessed the seventh day and made it
a holy day, because on that day he rested from all the
work he had done in creating the world.*

—Genesis 2:3 (NCV)

How can I remind myself that rest
is holy and necessary?

Year: _____

_____

_____

_____

_____

Year: _____

_____

_____

_____

_____

Year: _____

_____

_____

_____

_____

December 23

The hopes of the godly result in happiness,
but the expectations of the wicked come to nothing.
—Proverbs 10:28 (NLT)

What are my expectations for
Christmas? Are they godly?

Year: _____

_____
_____
_____
_____

Year: _____

_____
_____
_____
_____

Year: _____

_____
_____
_____
_____

December 24

*"For where two or three gather in my name,
there am I with them."*
—Matthew 18:20 (NIV)

Who will I gather with this week to celebrate
Jesus's presence in our lives?

Year: _____
_____
_____
_____
_____

Year: _____
_____
_____
_____
_____

Year: _____
_____
_____
_____
_____

December 25

And she brought forth her firstborn Son...and laid Him in a manger, because there was no room for them in the inn.
—Luke 2:7 (NKJV)

What do I need to put aside to make more
room in my heart for Jesus?

Year: _____

_____
_____
_____
_____

Year: _____

_____
_____
_____
_____

Year: _____

_____
_____
_____
_____

December 26

*When they saw the star, they rejoiced
with exceedingly great joy.*
—Matthew 2:10 (NKJV)

When have I clearly received
a sign from You?

Year: _____

_____

_____

_____

_____

Year: _____

_____

_____

_____

_____

Year: _____

_____

_____

_____

_____

December 27

"You will rest in his love;
he will sing and be joyful about you."
—Zephaniah 3:17b (NCV)

When have I felt completely embraced by You?
How can I have that experience more?

Year: _____

_____

_____

_____

_____

Year: _____

_____

_____

_____

_____

Year: _____

_____

_____

_____

_____

December 28

*"I will take out your stony, stubborn heart
and give you a tender, responsive heart."*
—Ezekiel 36:26b (NLT)

When am I most stubborn and least
responsive to You?

Year: _____

_____
_____
_____
_____

Year: _____

_____
_____
_____
_____

Year: _____

_____
_____
_____
_____

December 29

*"For Yours is the kingdom and the power
and the glory forever. Amen."*
—Matthew 6:13b (NKJV)

What is one situation in which I can recite these
words to keep my focus Your focus?

Year: _____

_____

_____

_____

_____

Year: _____

_____

_____

_____

_____

Year: _____

_____

_____

_____

_____

December 30

"Men of Galilee," they said, "why do you stand here looking into the sky?"
—Acts 1:11a (NIV)

In what situation am I standing and looking into the sky when I need to take action?

Year: _____

_____

_____

_____

_____

Year: _____

_____

_____

_____

_____

Year: _____

_____

_____

_____

_____

December 31

"For I know the plans I have for you," says the LORD. "They are plans for good and not for disaster, to give you a future and a hope."
—Jeremiah 29:11 (NLT)

What do You want me to know
about my future?

Year: _____

_____
_____
_____
_____

Year: _____

_____
_____
_____
_____

Year: _____

_____
_____
_____
_____